TRUE LOVE REVEALED

A Journey of Discovery

By Diana M. Sykes

Donated by
Christian Library International
Box 97095 Raleigh NC 2762.
Sign up for the CLI Bible St
Tell us how this book helped

Rocket Your Faith Series: Volume 1

Copyright © 2008 Diana M. Sykes

TRUE LOVE REVEALED

Rocket Your Faith Series Volume 1.

Printed in the United States of America

All rights reserved. No part of this publication may be reproduced or transmitted in any form or by any means without written permission of the author.

BIBLE VERSIONS USED:

The Holy Bible, New Century Version.
Copyright © 1987, 88,91 by Word Publishing.

The Ryrie Study Bible, N.I.V. Version,
Copyright 1986. By Moody Press

The Amplfied Bible Expanded Edition. Copyright © 1987 by Zondervan Corp. & The Lockman Press.

Spirit Filled Life Bible. Copyright © 1991 by Thomas Nelson Inc.

The Holy Bible. New King James Version.
Copyright © 1982 by Thomas Nelson Inc.

Holy Bible, New Living Translation. Copyright © 1996, 2004 Tynedale House Publishers.

EXTRACTS TAKEN FROM:

Molecules of Emotion,, Candace B. Pert, PH.D, Copyright 1997

Make the Most of Your Mind, Tony Buzan, Copyright 1984

The New Strong's Expanded Concordance, James Strong, LL.D.,, S.T.D. Copyright 2001

CONTENTS

References

Contents

Acknowledgements

Introduction

Chapter		Page
1	God, the truth about His Character	1
2	What you don't know will hurt you!	4
3	The Secret to experiencing true love	6
4	Do you feel wounded or wanted?	10
5	Priority Letters: What will you do with them?	14
6	Perception: True or not, it is working for or against you	20
7	Your days of being "conned" can be over!	22
8	Are you living the "lie" or the life?	24
9	Oppression versus Love	29
10	Knowledge is power...but only if you use it!	34
11	The Word of God is an internal mirror!	38
12	What are your thoughts telling you today?	43
13	Time for a fresh new mental attitude?	48
14	Pull out the bitter roots	52
15	Where did that come from?	56
16	What an amazing gift: Peace of mind and heart!	58
17	Life and Death are in the power of the tongue	62
18	Lighten your load and unlock your burdens	67
19	Are you captive to your thoughts?	72

Life-Shaping Prayer Method	76
Salvation Prayer	79
Purchase Books	81

ACKNOWLEDGEMENTS

I am grateful for the inspiration and wisdom of so many men and women who have had a passion to see people experience more in life. These are people whom I have gleaned wisdom, insight and understanding that has helped me not only to get "more out of life" but have enabled me to use the tools I have learned from them to help others as well.

I want to thank my husband, Gerald and son, Alan, who assisted in the editing of this book, because there is so much to be said about the "Revealed Love of God" that I have had difficulty knowing when to stop!

Thanks to so many of my friends that kept urging me to get "it" finished so they could share the principles with others.

Thanks to all the wonderful people who provided the Testimonies that will open the door to change in others' lives as well.

But, most of all, thanks to the Father, the Son and the Holy Spirit who gave me the chance to live life and live it more abundantly!

INTRODUCTION

This book and the information contained in it can be your breakthrough to a happier more productive life. I challenge you to take this book and USE IT! It will assist you in taking back into your own hands the responsibility for your destiny and your true identity and enable you to release the awesome potential within you.

With that in mind, it is good to remember that there have been many noble and wise men and women that have been instrumental in our lives; however, always keep in mind that only One Man suffered and died so that you could have the opportunity to experience the life God desires for you to live in the here and now and for eternity. To continue to have your life detoured and diverted by individuals that have not been properly connected to the love of God, is simply not taking into account what Jesus willingly did on your behalf.

Today could be the beginning of the best days of your life!

Chapter 1
God, the truth about His Character

Love is about the CHARACTER of the One giving the love.

This truth sets the standard for this book! This book is for you if you have ever questioned what your purpose is for being on the earth and/or why so many disconcerting events have happened to you along the way. It is about getting you back to the beginning where the first thought of you was ever conceived. It is about answers that can set you free from years of stored up hang ups! Then, it is about restoration. It is about a fresh new experience with the One that loves you and created you for that love.

This book could very well be the missing piece of the puzzle that you have been searching for. It is based on faith—faith in God, the truth about His Character and His promises to man that are manifested through the person of Jesus Christ. God went to such an extreme measure to give you an opportunity to know Him and EXPERIENCE His True Love and once you are able to comprehend this, I believe you will never be the same. Get ready to be changed!

The true character of God and His love are powerfully expressed in **Romans 5:8** which states the following:

"But God shows and clearly proves His [own] love for us by the fact that while we were still sinners Christ, the Messiah, the Anointed One, died for us."

The purpose for Jesus coming to earth was to make His Father's love known. We needed a Savior to show us the way back to the Father and His love. We cannot earn God's love. It is a gift that is available to everyone who will receive it! The price paid for us to experience the gift of God's love was astronomical!

No matter what your experiences have been from birth until now, the Lord's greatest desire is that you would experience the incredible love that He proved by sending His Son to die for you so that you could be reconnected to

Him...a loving Heavenly Father and so that you could have knowledge to be able to live the absolute life He created you to live.

HOW OFTEN HAS THE SINCERITY OF YOUR LOVE BEEN QUESTIONED?

Have you ever had a situation where you loved someone and endeavored to do the very best for them and your intentions were either misunderstood, taken lightly or brushed aside? Think how the Lord must feel when He has clearly demonstrated how much He loves us, yet so many have misunderstood or have not studied to become knowledgeable of His true intentions for them and His desire, not only for their eternal life with Him, but their abundant life in the here and now!

FREEDOM OF CHOICE – ONE OF GOD'S GREATEST GIFTS!

Because the truth about the love of God has been watered down, many people have chosen and/or accepted an altered belief system but God so loves them that He continues to give them the freedom of choice; while, at the same time, He sets up circumstances and people of faith to come into their path so they could be prodded to look for His truth.

Think about the worse day or time in your life when you may have experienced strife, confusion, anxiety, feelings of rejection and felt totally misunderstood and disillusioned! If you knew there was someone that had made a way for your life to change, wouldn't you want to take time to find out what you needed to know so that your life would begin changing for the better?

For years I experienced so much of the negativity mentioned above until the day I answered an altar call to accept Jesus, the Son of God, as my Savior at an evangelistic service. I was full of fear and trepidation because I really didn't know what to expect. I just knew I needed a change and the change that the evangelist was speaking of. After my conversion I sought God diligently because I loved Him. I remember the day I received Christ as my Savior, it was as if the air and atmosphere around me changed. Even so, I had so much junk stored in my soul that it took years for me to realize and to experience how much God loves me personally. I began to take time to find out what He had to say about His intentions for me while at the same time I was discarding memories of life's issues that sought to continue to control my present and that were blocking the future that He had planned for me. I was a work in progress, and for that part, continue to be! Thank God I now have an exciting revelation that I am here for a purpose, His purpose, and He enjoys me as He watches me grow from faith to faith each day.

Chapter 2
What you don't know will hurt you!

HAVE YOU EVER HEARD THE SAYING, "WHAT YOU DON'T KNOW WON'T HURT YOU?

THAT STATEMENT IS ONE OF THE BIGGEST LIES EVER TOLD!

UNTIL YOU LEARN AND HEAR THE TRUTH ABOUT THE TRUE LOVE OF GOD AND THE GIFT OF HIS SON WHO OFFERS YOU ETERNAL LIFE, YOU WILL BE LIVING THE LIE, NOT THE LIFE HE PLANNED FOR YOU. THAT LACK OF KNOWLEDGE WILL DEFINITELY HURT YOU!

Prayerfully the truths you will learn about God, and what I have found about His true character, can set you free so that you can begin to enjoy His true love and the life experiences He desires for you.

Why did it take me so long to experience and enjoy my Heavenly Father's love? I believe the answer lies in the fact that I related to people, places and things based on my life's experiences. I needed an experience with His truth and His unconditional love.

DO YOU HAVE GOD'S LOVE CONFUSED WITH PEOPLES' LOVE?

Through years of talking with, ministering to and observing people, I have found the common denominator in peoples' lives is the need for love, acceptance, and something as simple, but, oh so big, as being understood!

How many people do you know who are comfortable with who they are and secure in the knowledge of how much they are loved by God and have a purpose to fulfill? As we will discuss in greater length, most of us base our feelings about God and ourselves on what others say and how they act towards us rather than on the truth. As you read and study this book, I pray the "real" you that is so loved by God will begin to experience the realness of the abundant love He has for you. I pray that you will "throw off" the false identity you may have assumed because of confusing peoples' love with God's love and realize how very much you are loved, accepted and understood! The best way to begin is to become aware that in the New Testament, God expresses His love, care, compassion, interest and will for our lives through Jesus Christ. "For God so loved the world that He gave His only begotten Son that whosoever would believe in Him would not perish but have everlasting life!" **John 3:16**

First of all, let's give thought to the fact that this Scripture begins with "For God so loved," and then, He tells us why accepting the way He showed that love is so important. He does not want us to perish. What does it mean then, that He does not want us to perish? Even though the literal translation of the word "perish" seems a bit extensive, its relevance is extremely important to understanding how much God cares and is interested in your well-being.

Understanding this truth has the potential to be life changing! The word "perish" actually means that God so much did not want us to lose our well-being, that He did not want us to miss out on a place with Him, that He sent His Son, His Love, to us and for us!

God wants you to accept His love and trust His promises so you can live successfully with a sense of well-being and safety. You see, all of mankind is a creation of God with a free will. When you freely accept His gift of love, His Son as Savior, you are not only His creation, but you become His child.

Chapter 3
The Secret to experiencing true love

HAVE YOU EVER WISHED THAT SOMEONE WOULD REALLY LISTEN?

How many times have you so deeply wanted to help a family member or friend out of a bad situation and you felt such a strong need to do whatever it took to get them to a place of safety?   They, of course, had to be willing to listen to you and accept your help.

In a similar way, to the degree that you understand the fullness of this love God offers through Jesus Christ is the degree that His love and fullness of life will be experienced in your life on a daily basis. It is important to Him that you do not miss out on this love!

The secret to experiencing true love is in getting rid of preconceived ideas about God and learning the truths about what your life means to Him. Once you have read and digested the truth about God's true love for you, 'what it is and what it isn't,' you will never again have to feel like a pawn on a game board, but you will know for sure that you are purposefully designed to be here and there is no one else like you in all the earth. Isn't that a wonderful but awesome thought?

Unfortunately, this truth has been kept a secret because most people, including many Christians, have accepted "natural" or "worldly" love as the basis for their belief system of what love is. In other words, they have based their very life purpose on what life has dealt them. Until you explore and experience the fact that God's intentions for you are pure, good, lovely, true and of a good report, you will never be able to experience the quality of life He planned for you to live. It is vitally important that you understand that His love is constant. God's character is to love and, as a Christian, that love character is transferred to your spirit! However, your soul needs freeing from the worldly or negative beliefs and "stuff" which have accumulated over the years.

One of the most powerful Scriptures in the Bible is **III John 1:2**

"Beloved I wish above all things that you would prosper and be in health even as your SOUL prospers."

Above all things the Lord wants you to have your soul reconditioned to understand all He has in store for you on your journey in life. This book is about learning how to get your soul restored so that you can experience His wishes and desires for you, which, He says, are health and prosperity and well-being! Does that seem too good to be true? If so, read the above Scripture again. If you find it hard to believe, do not worry; this only means you need your soul reconditioned to the truth and you need to let go of the things that have conditioned you to think other wise!

ARE YOU STUCK IN A RUT?

There is a way to get unstuck! If you are ready for a change in your life, begin now by praying and asking the Lord to show you areas where you have confused His love with mankind's love. It is also very important for you to think about the character of the person or persons that caused you to have an altered sense of who you are. If you often find yourself feeling rejected or unacceptable, ask Him to show you what specific event or events caused these feelings. Be open and honest with yourself and zoom in on the "issues" that you seem to be confronted with over and over that hinder you on a regular basis. You are looking for the truth that will get you on track with where you need to be. On Page 76 I have included a **Life Shaping Prayer Method** that will assist you.

This exercise is significant and can be a turning point in your life. Get a pen and paper and write down what comes to your mind!

It could be something that seems very insignificant to you but could be the very thing that can get you "unstuck" so that you can experience soul renewal. This part of cleansing your soul, our Scripture states, clearly will begin opening the door to prosperity and health and wholeness. God says your "soul" is a key to answered prayer.

Be aware of what feels uncomfortable when you think about it. Do not filter or reject any thoughts that come up. Accept the fact that Jesus wants to show you exactly what you need to know so that you can fully accept how much He and His Father care for you. As we will study in more detail, when your soul is renewed, "rivers of living water" that spring up to "new life" that Jesus spoke about in **John 7:38** can begin to flow through you. Think about it, He did say "new life." The real you that is full of potential and vitality can begin to come forth. You will feel much more emotionally free and able to accept God's love for you. This will help you deal in a more peaceful way with issues that have troubled you in the past! This is when the promise in **III John** can truly BEGIN to be realized. In that Scripture, He calls you His Beloved. What a powerful term of endearment as He expresses His wish and desire for your health and prosperity no matter what you have experienced in the past.

An easy illustration to help you understand how this works is as follows: Some years ago I had a sports car that I had put a new battery in. However, because it had sat for quite some time afterwards without being started or driven, the cables that connected to the battery became corroded so that when I finally did decide to start the car, the battery could not release the power because of the corrosion. The battery had the power but the connection could not be made until the corrosion was removed. Then, one turn of the switch and all was well.

Life's events can clog and corrode your soul so that you cannot fully accept the life God has planned for you. Just like the car was "stuck" and not going anywhere, our lives seemingly get stuck in a frustrating rut. Taking time to get rid of these blocks can open up the way for fresh new beginnings for you.

I remember a woman that took time to go through the **Life Shaping Prayer Method** (pg. 76) who had been so wounded by events that happened in her life between she and her husband. She was very hurt, shamed, angry and disillusioned with life even though she spent hours studying the Bible. After she was able to release the wounds caused by her husband leaving her, she was able to accept that there were major things he was involved in which were opening the door to all kinds of bad things. She then became free indeed to experience God's love and feel confidence in the Lord. She no longer felt the Lord had let her down. He had actually set her free! In fact, after she had been through a few "sessions" of letting go of negative events, she went into the Residence Office where she lived and the Manager, who had not seen her for a while, said to her, "You look great and so rested, have you been on vacation?" Jesus came to set the captive free. Taking time to become aware of areas where you are being held captive in your soul is part of His wonderful work on the Cross for you! When she got the blocks/chains that had controlled her soul removed her countenance showed it! The Lord wants to do the same for you.

"Blessed is the man who finds wisdom, the man who gains understanding." **Proverbs 3:13**

This wisdom the Lord wants to reveal to you will give you understanding not only about yourself but about others that have touched your life. You will be empowered to make better decisions about your life NOW as opposed to carrying baggage and wrong ideas and misunderstandings into your future.

Wisdom, according to this Scripture is something you look for—you must find it! Wisdom comes when you seek it; so let's be on a search and find mission for a true perspective of God's desire for your blessed, prosperous life. Becoming aware of God's wisdom for you will enable you to become a winner in the midst of a world filled with obstacles.

Chapter 4
Do you feel wounded or wanted?

DO YOU KNOW HOW MUCH YOU ARE WANTED?

Ephesians 1:5 "In love, He predestined us to be adopted as His sons through Jesus Christ, in accordance with His pleasure and will..."

Take a moment to put your name in this Scripture. "In love, He predestined (your name) to be adopted as His sons [and daughters] through Jesus Christ, in accordance with His pleasure and will!

IT HAS ALWAYS BEEN GOD'S PLEASURE AND WILL TO BLESS YOU!

When you become born again through faith in Jesus Christ and accept Him as your Lord and Savior, one of the many benefits He has for you is that you are adopted by Father God! This Scripture says that it gives Him pleasure to have you as His son or daughter. It has always been God's will to bless you! Notice it says, "In love, He predestined you to be adopted..." He wanted you back....God never liked being separated from you. When Adam and Eve failed to trust the power of His love and truth, they became separated from all He had in store for them. They began to perish. It was a choice!

FOOD FOR THOUGHT!

SOMEONE ELSE MAY HAVE MADE CHOICES FOR YOU IN THE BEGINNING AND AT DIFFERENT TIMES IN YOUR LIFE, BUT THE GREAT NEWS IS, NOW, YOU HAVE THE CHOICE TO MAKE RIGHT DECISIONS SO THAT WHAT YOU NOW CHOOSE WILL HAVE A POSITIVE INFLUENCE ON YOUR LIFE AS WELL ON OTHERS' LIVES!

As stated above, others' choices trickled down through mankind and that is why God sent Jesus to give us the opportunity to make the choice of reconnecting with His love. Truly realizing this and accepting the fact that God wants us to be blessed and free indeed to enjoy the life in the here and now is our choice. Just as He made provision for us to be adopted so that we could experience the love of a caring Heavenly Father, we honor Him by accepting His love, care and fidelity to us. Your ability to trust Him is big on His priority list for you.

HAS LIFE COLORED YOUR ABILITY TO SEE CLEARLY?

This requires a change of mind for many of us who have had our ability to receive His love colored and hindered either by things we have experienced in life or lack of knowledge of how much He cares for us. So many have grown up in dysfunctional situations and have been surrounded by family and friends who have experienced emotional upheaval and have never really understood how to get free from all the negative effects this has had on their lives.

I can certainly speak from experience because I grew up in a very dysfunctional environment. I have a deep respect and incredible love for my parents, who became born-again after my brother, sister and I left home. However, the negative effects of my parent's childhood and how they were treated had a dramatically negative effect not only on their lives but our lives as well. In fact, my Dad recently commented after my Mom passed away, "We brought so much baggage and pain into our marriage and life and never fully got to experience what life should have been for us." This book is about helping people, like my Mom, Dad and our family, break free from ancestral issues, lies, ungodly beliefs and habit patterns that caused cycles of defeat in their lives and our lives, which God had no part in.

My parents were diligent hardworking people who taught us as children a good work ethic. However, because my parents had not experienced the Presence and true love of God in their home in their growing up years, they did not realize for many years how important it was in raising a family to put effort into learning and subsequently teaching us about the love and purposes of God and giving Him first place in our home and lives.

Again, this was because they had taken on board so many issues that caused hurt from their parents in the form of wounded emotions, lack of love, strife, angry outbursts, rejection, lack of validation, etc., and subsequently passed it on to us in so many ways.

ARE YOU A CANDIDATE FOR GETTING RID OF DOWNLINE FAMILY "STUFF?"

I must say that my Mother prayed, studied and sought God diligently after she became born again. She volunteered her time to work phone banks to pray for peoples' needs and she led many to the Lord! I believe her prayers are still making a significant difference in our lives and others today. My Dad, as well, is now a man of prayer for his family.

Prayerfully this book will make you become more aware that painful, negative "stuff" that you may have experienced, as my family did, was a result of generations not being properly connected to God or understanding His true character and love. You can begin a new solid foundation for those you love and care for by getting rid of the results of past ancestral failures, ungodly beliefs and feelings of rejection that have caused so many family failures.

The Bible teaches us to "Cast off (which means to hurl away) those weights and sins that so easily beset us (get us off course), and to look unto Jesus, the Author and Finisher of our faith!" **Hebrews 12: 1&2**

It is God's desire that you experience His love and pass it on to others. However, you can only give to others what you have experienced yourself! Thank God you no longer will have to just assume "this is just the way it is" and live life carrying baggage that doesn't belong to you. Negative mindsets, habits and ignorance of the power of the Word of God and His True Love can be a thing of the past for you.

ARE YOU READY TO BE THE ONE THAT SETS A HIGHER STANDARD FOR FUTURE GENERATIONS IN YOUR FAMILY AND YOUR SPHERE OF INFLUENCE?

Are you ready to be launched into a happier more vibrant life? Have you ever read the powerful words Jesus spoke in **Mark 9:23:** "If YOU can believe, all things are possible to those that will believe?"

"Believe" actually means "to have faith in." So, if you can accept and have total faith in the fact that Jesus words are true and you implement them into your life's circumstances, changes will invariably be the result! That is good news and God is no respecter of persons but He is a respecter of faith in those that trust Him and His Word.

Realizing that God chose you to be adopted so that you can be a part of His family and truly becoming aware that He did not want you to miss out on experiencing true love and a sense of well-being will help you readdress how you may be feeling about yourself, your loved ones and those that have touched your life.

Chapter 5
Priority Letters: What will you do with them?

NOW IS A GOOD TIME TO BEGIN LIVING
THE LIFE GOD INTENDED FOR YOU TO LIVE!

When you become born again by accepting Jesus into your heart and confessing that Jesus is Lord, you become joint heirs with Jesus. The Bible says He actually becomes your elder brother and you are an heir to all the promises that God made to Jesus because you are now a part of His family. As you read the Bible where you will learn what rightly belongs to you, see it not just as a "good" book, but as "Priority Letters" to you which hold information you need to move forward daily in life with wisdom and insight.

Because of a lack of understanding of how deeply they are loved by their Heavenly Father, many have lived far beneath the privileges God has established in His Word for them. They have let so much accumulated "stuff" control their lives.

If our Creator said in **John 10:10**, "I came that you might have life and have it (life) more abundantly," shouldn't that be what we base our faith and trust in rather than what life has dealt many of us, or what others may have said to or about us?

It has been stated that we have three identities:

1. Who people say we are;
2. Who we have become because of what we have accepted as the truth based on what others have said or done to us, and,
3. Who we are, based on who Christ says we are!

A fresh experience with God's love and taking time to get release from preconceived ideas, hurts and others' opinions that have been stored in your soul can connect you to the identity Christ paid for you to have. You, yes, you have so much in store when you accept the truth about how much you are loved! Jesus said "abundant life" was His goal for you!

To be more specific as to what Jesus was saying when He said His desire for you was abundant life, some of the meanings from the Greek language which give a more complete picture are: "Advantage," "What is above and over, superadded", "What is superior and advantageous," "In a more super-abundant way," and "Exceedingly and out of measure."

I Timothy 2:4 states that "It is God's desire that all men be saved and come into the knowledge of the truth."

IF WE NEED TO "COME INTO THE KNOWLEDGE OF THE TRUTH," THERE MUST BE MANY UNTRUTHS OR LIES TO GET RID OF!

The work of salvation covers every area of life and to receive the fullness of it, you have to pursue His truths and act on them in the here and now! When we become born again, our spirits are reconnected to God but our souls have to be renewed day by day to fulfill what God has planned for us. Getting "rid" of untruths opens the door wide for knowledge of the truth to come in! He desires you to know you have a safe place in Him. He is concerned that you experience the feeling of well-being and care knowing you are loved by your Heavenly Father.

The world is a confusing place and the Bible says in the latter days people will lose consideration for each other because of pressures all around but, He has promised a Covenant of love that cannot be altered and the more you learn of His love the more you will experience His higher purpose for you, which He states is health, prosperity and well-being...not what you may have experienced or are experiencing today.

HE EVEN WANTS TO REWARD YOU FOR SEEKING HIM BECAUSE IT GIVES HIM SUCH PLEASURE TO SEE YOU LIVING IN HIS BLESSINGS!

I pray that this book will help you experience the blessings God has stored up for you and that it will help you to understand the "great exchange" you need to make on a daily basis to incorporate and experience God's promises and truths in your life.

GOD IS AN EQUAL OPPORTUNITY GOD!

He says in **Hebrews 11:6**, "Without faith it is impossible to please Him, for He that comes to God must believe that He is, and that He is a Rewarder of those that diligently seek Him."

Are you willing to be one of the "THOSE THAT DILIGENTLY SEEK HIM" that He is speaking about? You have to seek Him for yourself. He says, "You must realize He is" and that He has you on His mind for a purpose. If you have depended on others' perception of God, you may have missed out on a lot of things already. It is never too late to begin believing for yourself that "He is" and that He wants to reward your faith in Him and His promises. Also take time daily to think about what and who you have been basing your faith in to see if it warrants your continued focus!

MAN'S OPINIONS OR GOD'S OPINIONS, WHICH WILL YOU CHOOSE?

The issues most of us have are that we have put more confidence in man and his opinions than we have in what God has said. Again, it is very empowering to realize God has a reward for those that take time to get to know Him for who He really is and commit to applying His principles in their daily lives so that they can bear fruit in their life.

YOU ARE DEEMED A PERSON OF VALUE BY GOD!

It pleases Him when you realize how much you are "deemed" a person of value and cared for by Him. The great thing for everyone to realize is that when they are born again, He gifts each and everyone with "the measure of faith" – **Romans 12:3.**

Everyone starts off with the same measure of faith, however, to increase your measure of faith you need to know that the God kind of faith that opens the door to experiencing true love, prosperity and wholeness "Comes by hearing and hearing by the Word of God" according to **Romans 10:17.**

THINK ABOUT YOUR LIFE TODAY, HOW MUCH OF THE WORD OF GOD DO YOU HEAR ON A CONSISTENT BASIS?

HOW MUCH HAVE YOU HEARD OVER YOUR LIFE TIME?

NOW, TAKE TIME TO THINK OF HOW MANY WORDS FROM "MAN" YOU HEAR ON A REGULAR BASIS AND HOW MUCH YOU HAVE HEARD OVER YOUR LIFETIME....WHICH ONE IS NOW HAVING THE GREATEST INFLUENCE IN YOUR LIFE?

Psalms 1, for instance, tells us how blessed we will be when we seek His counsel and meditate on His Words rather than sitting around listening to the ungodly or those that are scornful or not properly connected to God. His promise to us is that "if" we stay focused, whatever we would put our hand to would prosper in its season and appointed time. He says that we would be "like" trees planted by rivers of water that would produce fruit in its season.

This means, of course, you need to be actively seeking His wisdom for you and not sitting passively and accepting what the "world" has to say about you and your circumstances. A case in point is Television, Internet, Radio, Newsprint, and Peoples' conversation in general, these can very easily usurp time and often provide information that is not *faith-filled*, but more often than not, *fear-filled*.

His desire is for you to "seek FIRST His kingdom and His righteousness" so that He can ADD all things to you according to Jesus' words in **Matthew 6:33**! This "ADDING" comes as a result of your faith being activated and exercised with confidence in how much He loves and cares for you. When He speaks of "meditating" in Psalms 1, this word actually means "to speak out over and over." That is how you activate God's word in your life which will open the door to abundant life! I encourage you to be aware of whose words you are speaking and who is there to back them up.

DO YOU THINK GOD IS ANGRY WITH YOU?

One of the reasons people do not receive the love God has for them is because they think God is angry at them. Many base their faith and confidence in God on their experiences with their earthly father, relatives or other authority figures or even they have based their beliefs on others' perception of God instead of taking time to get to know Him personally.

Could that be you? The truth is, however, we were created to be objects of His love and care so that we, in turn, could be a blessing to Him and share His love, truths, and blessings with others. Always remember, "For God so loved that He gave".....and He has not changed His mind or His nature. He is still giving. The question is: "Are you receiving?"

So that you can more fully understand how much God desires you to be a whole, complete person, free from the world's standards of life, let's explore what Jesus came to earth to do for you, as an individual.

JESUS WAS ON A MISSION FOR MANKIND!

In **Luke 4:18-19**, Jesus said, "The Spirit of the Lord is upon Me, because he has anointed Me to preach the good news (the Gospel) to the poor, he has sent me to heal the brokenhearted, to proclaim liberty to the captives and recovery of sight to the blind, to set at liberty those who are oppressed; to proclaim the acceptable year of the Lord."

The word "blind" in the above Scripture is used metaphorically to mean "dulling of the intellect" or "opaque." Jesus came to breathe passion, truth and clarity about how much God loves you and places significance on you understanding it!

Let's face it! Jesus came to bring good news, not bad news! This clearly says that Jesus came to set people free from hurts, wounds, emotional stress and bondages brought on by a fallen world that had been disconnected from a loving God and who had been held captive by lies and deception. He is still doing this through revelation of truth which will bring light to your mind, will and emotions so that the "opaqueness" will go.

MANY RELIGIONS PORTRAY GOD AS AN ANGRY GOD AND CONSEQUENTLY PROCLAIM MORE "BAD NEWS" THAN "GOOD NEWS!"

If God were angry at you or had caused all of these conflicts why would He have sent His Son to suffer and die to get you restored and healed of the painful issues and circumstances in your life? Why would He have sent Jesus to talk with you about the way to get emotionally healed and His way to experience freedom in every area of life? Why would He have sent Him to take the blinders off of your mind so that you could live a "free indeed" life with happiness and contentment which brings glory to Him?

Jesus said He came to set the captives free, not to add more pressure in peoples' lives! The word "captive" means prisoner of war. The war is between truth and lies, good and evil. Jesus came to set you free from lies and the evil around you so that you could experience the life God intended for you from the beginning. This is all a part of "coming into the knowledge of the truth" after salvation. **Genesis 1:26** and **27**, says, "You were made in the image and likeness of God." That has to be good!

HOW DO WE GET FROM WHERE WE ARE NOW TO WHERE THE LORD WANTS US TO BE, WHICH IS, "FREE INDEED" ACCORDING TO **JOHN 8:36**

We must first realize that our soul, which includes our mind, will and emotions, has been programmed from birth with ancestral, social and cultural thought patterns and experiences. You today are carrying the happenings of yesterday with you. Because of this, most people continue living out what they have experienced, and what has been passed down to them, without even realizing that is what they are doing. Today, however, you can begin making the great exchange, which is ....God's thoughts and intentions for you to replace the ancestral, social, and cultural thought patterns and experiences that have led you into a frustrated or mediocre life. You can begin living the abundant, creative, productive life Jesus, our Savior, spoke about. This is what renewing the mind is about.

Chapter 6
Perception: True or not, it is working for or against you?

A TRANSFORMED, RENEWED MIND THINKS GOD THOUGHTS!

In **Mark 8:36** Jesus says, "For what will it profit a man if he gains the whole world and loses his own soul?"

How many people do you know who are greatly successful outwardly but inwardly have no peace or true contentment? Many people around the world apply God-inspired principles but do not know the Author of those principles personally and His desire for a true love connection with them now and for eternity.

If you just live your life based on your experiences and never get to know the Savior and live out His purposes, you will miss out on the reason for being on this earth. In fact, I heard someone make this very profound statement once: "That man was more valuable than the entire earth because, the Bible says the earth will pass away but man's spirit will live forever."

Think about it! You are an eternal being. Earth is a place you are only passing through. Eternity is forever! Jesus said in **John 17:3** "Now, this is eternal life: that they may know you, the only true God, and Jesus Christ whom you have sent."

God wants the truth of His intentions to be what lead you rather than the pattern the natural world has set for you. Take a few minutes to think about how important this is to the Lord that you know and experience how special you, as an individual, are to Him.

YOUR LIFE IS A JOURNEY. IF YOU HAVE HAD DIFFICULTIES TODAY, GROWING IN THE KNOWLEDGE OF THE TRUTH WILL HELP YOUR JOURNEY BE BETTER TOMORROW!

He truly desires you to have success on your journey in life and has provided the way for this to happen. This book is about encouraging you to **establish** new thinking and habit patterns. It will encourage you to rightly divide God's Word so that old patterns, habits and assumptions about who you are can be released from you.

If you get rid of the old thoughts about yourself and begin living God's thoughts about who you are, you will become much more confident and enthusiastic about life!

RENEWING YOUR MIND WITH GOD'S TRUTHS WAS SO IMPORTANT TO THE APOSTLE PAUL THAT HE ACTUALLY BEGGED AND PLEADED WITH PEOPLE TO RENEW THEIR MINDS ON A REGULAR BASIS.

How important is it that you do this?

Let's look intently at Paul's words to the church in **Romans 12**: He said, "I beg and urge you, because of the mercies of God, that you not be conformed to this world, but be transformed by the renewing of your mind so that you can know the good, acceptable and perfect will of God for you."

Now, if someone that I trusted came to me today and said to me, "I beg you not to keep doing this or that because if you keep doing this, you will be stuck in a rut." And then, what if they would say to me, "If you change the way you think, the sky will be the limit," and, of course, I knew them to be of great character, I would be foolish not to do something about what they are saying!

Through the Apostle Paul, God is saying the same thing to us. He is saying trust me in this. I do have a perfect plan for you. I want you to become aware of how much you are loved and when you realize how much love and mercy I have in store for you, you will be on your way to experiencing the good, acceptable and perfect will of God. This means a more productive abundant life. You will be able to let go of your old way of thinking and habit patterns that have led to frustration and roadblocks and begin experiencing your true purpose for being on this earth, which is to live out God's perfect will just for you!

Chapter 7
Your days of being "conned" can be over!

HAVE YOU BEEN CONNED?

To get a clearer picture, I like to break down the word "conformed" like this: Do not be "conned" and "formed" by what your experiences or people have said you have to be. To be conned means to be tricked, swindled, deceived and reasoned against. To be conformed also means to become adapted to general customs and patterns. These thought patterns have formed who you are today. These thought patterns have been based on things going on around you that you have accepted as status quo!

IF GOD PUTS GREAT EMPHASIS ON HOW YOU THINK AND WHAT YOU THINK, SHOULDN'T YOU?

God's emphasis on the need to change how you think is vital to Him and to you so that you will not miss out on all He created you to be. So many people do miss out on the goodness God has for them because of faulty thinking. Will you determine not to be one of those?

I'M NOT SAYING IT IS EASY, BUT THE REWARDS ARE WORTH THE EFFORT!

So, to reiterate, this is what being transformed by the renewing of your mind means: Let go of what you have become based on the world's pattern and your experiences and learn who He created you to be. He says that is His desire for you to know His perfect will so why not determine every day that you will experience not only His acceptable and good, but His perfect will for you! So, you may be asking, "How do I really do this so that I can experience life more fully?

WHOSE VOICE ARE YOU HEARING AND ACTING ON?

In **Hebrews 3:7**, God said, "Today, if you hear my voice, do not harden your heart! In other words, stay receptive and tender every day looking for truths from God and His Word! Do you know what happens when you go a few days without physical food? You get weak. The same is true with your soul. Think how strong you could become if you ate spiritual food from the Word of God and fed your soul on a regular basis and applied this knowledge to every area of your life!

Jesus made an astounding statement, "He said the words I speak are spirit and they are life." **John 6:63.**

In other words, His words impacted His environment in a positive way. Yours can too! In fact, take a look at your life today and think about what words have impacted you that you have accepted as the truth, but are they? If you have had failures and mistakes over and over in your life, often you will have a tendency to believe and say things like "nothing good ever happens to me" or "there is no use trying," etc. If this is the case, you need an emotional house cleaning to get rid of the mind pollution that will keep you in a cycle of defeat. That is why, even in the midst of people calling Him names and hurling accusations against Him, He said He always spoke spirit and life!

To live and experience the true prosperity and success in life that God desires, you must be aware of the way Jesus dealt with issues that confronted Him. His attitude in the face of opposing forces is the example you are to follow? There is one thing for sure, if you do not know the methods the opposing forces use, it will be very difficult to lead the life God intends for you.

Chapter 8
Are you living the "lie" or the life?

THERE ARE TWO KINGDOMS – THE KINGDOM OF DARKNESS AND THE KINGDOM OF LIGHT!

Let us first realize that the name "Satan" in Hebrew means, "The arch-enemy of good, an adversary or plotter and an accuser." He is the prince of the Kingdom of Darkness.

Revelation 12:10 says that "He, Satan, accuses us before our God day and night." This Scripture indicates that Satan is on the job "24/7."

Satan constantly works to make us think wrong thoughts about God and His purpose for our life. He does this through subtle thoughts, suggestions and accusations, and he manipulates people around us to say things contrary to what God's desires are in order to bring havoc and confusion into our minds and lives. Satan works 24/7 to block the truth. If you are not aware of Satan's negative method of operating, you will miss out on the blessings that God has for you because you will find yourself assuming that "this is just the way it is."

SATAN USES THE SAME METHODS WITH US THAT HE DID WITH JESUS!

The good news is, Jesus defeated Satan for us and gave us power and authority to reject the lies and insinuations sent to us by the enemy and his forces. Jesus came to be our example of how to resist thoughts, suggestions and lies that are sent continually to hinder our lives. Satan's intentions are to keep us from running the race that would bring glory to God and bring us joy in life.

The Bible declares that when we become born-again Christians, we get transferred out of the "Kingdom of Darkness" into the "Kingdom of His dear Son." **Colossians 1:12 & 13.**

THIS WAS A POWERFUL TRANSFER BECAUSE IT GIVES YOU THE POTENTIAL TODAY THROUGH FAITH TO RECEIVE ALL THAT JESUS PAID THE AWESOME PRICE FOR.

SATAN NO LONGER HAS POWER OVER YOU, BUT YOU MUST DO SOMETHING WITH THIS TRUTH FOR IT TO WORK FOR YOU!

Our situation in all of this is the fact that, although we get "born again," which means our spirit is reborn, reconnected to God, our soul that contains our mind, will and emotions is still connected to all of our experiences. As we seek Jesus through His word, he will cleanse us of our hurtful experiences that keep us connected to ancestral issues and ungodly thought patterns that keep us in bondage to all sorts of fears, worries and doubts about ourselves. This includes "stuff" that we have taken on board when the "Kingdom of Darkness" had authority to rule over our lives.

When we focus on Jesus' promises and exchange His truths for the lies we have been living, we will begin to be free to enjoy the blessings God intends for us. Our minds must be "renewed" on a daily basis. As we read God's promises we will start to see ourselves as God sees us and not be ruled by our past experiences or failures.

THOUGHTS, WORDS, SUGGESTIONS –HAVE YOU BEEN THROWN OFF COURSE BY OTHER PEOPLES' THOUGHTS, WORDS OR SUGGESTIONS?

Lest you think that thoughts, words and suggestions are a small thing, was it not a thought, word and suggestion that got our ancestors, Adam and Eve off course? In **Genesis 3:1**, Satan said to Eve, "Did God really say, 'You must not eat from any tree in the garden'?" They listened to the wrong source and acted on what they heard which was doubt about God's faithfulness. The end result was detrimental to them, their families and to us today!

My husband and I have ministered to people in all walks of life: the Medical Field, the Financial Arena, Chief Executive Officers, Entrepreneurs, Pastors, Housewives, Therapists, Counselors, Friends, you name it.

What we have found is this: It does not matter what their level of success or education, when people have painful events, often from early childhood and/or other negative influences in their lives, and these "issues" have not been recognized or properly dealt with, these events have caused many to constantly live with feelings of abandonment, self-rejection, shame, fears, low self-esteem, anger, depression, sadness, and overwhelming feelings of never being able to measure up to parents, relatives, business associates or friends.

The consequence of all of this is feeling pressured by life. They are often smiling on the outside, but sad and feeling unsettled on the inside. Many are driven without peace! There is a void in their life that cannot and has not been filled by their outward circumstances or success.

As we go through life, our lives are influenced through relationships. If those relationships are not based on Godly principles, our self image will be greatly impacted which creates a void in our souls that needs to be filled with the truth.

A case in point is this: Just recently I was speaking with a therapist who told me his father, who as a young man had intended to go into ministry, was hitchhiking and the person who picked him up molested him. When he finally wrestled free and got out of the car, he went to a church vicar who slammed the door in his face, apparently because of his disheveled appearance! From that point on, he vowed he would never have anything else to do with God or the church!

God had nothing to do with the ill-treatment of this man. This was a life altered dramatically by people not properly connected to God! Not only did this severely alter his life' purpose and potentially people he may have brought to the Lord, but I was told he has physical infirmities as well that have kept him from fully enjoying life.

ARE YOU BLAMING GOD FOR SOMETHING SOMEONE LACKING IN CARE AND CONCERN HAS DONE?

Another case in point that affected my life, as well as my family in a dramatic way was my Dad, who has always been a very smart, intuitive, well read man. Early in his life, one of his school teachers recognized his zeal for learning and offered to pay his tuition to college. His Dad, however, disdainfully told him he was not any better than the other children and he would have to quit school and work like the rest of them. This event, among many others, caused anger, rage and resentment to build in my Dad that, unfortunately, was unleashed both verbally and physically on us as children and on my Mom as well for many years. He never had the experience in his early years of being nurtured and loved by his Dad, which is, of course, the opposite of what God would have desired for him. Nevertheless, this void of God's Presence in his home caused untold havoc in our home and subsequently our lives. I lived many of my early years in fear and dread. As mentioned before, he is now born again, loves the Lord and continues to grow in God's wisdom and worked hard taking care of my Mom before she passed away but, many of his and my Mom's generation have not been adequately able to release the heavy burdens placed on them in their early years and have remained stuck with the pain that Jesus said He bore for them.

The case in point is that we all have to be willing to be willing to give up and release our stored up pain to a Savior who bore this pain for us. Only then can we live a "free indeed" life that will make a mark on future generations.

As you are reading this book, anywhere you see yourself and desire to be free from the pain and blockages similar circumstances have caused you, take time to make notes of your memories and feelings. At the end of the book, I will share again ways for you to release these areas in your life so that you will no longer be conformed to what has happened to you. I believe you will be able to receive healing and experience the "well-being" I spoke of earlier that Jesus desires for you!

ARE YOU FORFEITING BREAKTHROUGHS GOD HAS PLANNED FOR YOU?

Can you imagine the number of people who are walking around with similar life altering experiences as my family and the therapists' father that have caused them to forfeit the blessings God has in store for them because individuals, not properly connected to God's love, acted in an abysmal way? Has your life been altered by wrong actions and choices of others? Jesus made the choice to die so that you might live in God's amazing love.

ONLY ONE MAN DIED SO THAT YOU COULD LIVE! DON'T YOU THINK IT WOULD BE A GREAT IDEA TO FIND OUT MORE ABOUT WHAT THIS MEANS TO YOU?

Always remember that only One Man, Jesus, died and suffered so that you could live the life God desires for you!

To continue to be diverted and detoured by individuals and their actions towards you is simply not taking into full consideration what Jesus suffered and conquered on your behalf. No one else did for you what He willingly did!

There is a powerful Scripture that says, "Do not take the mercy of God in vain!" **II Corinthians 6:1.**

In other words, consider how powerful His mercy is and give heed to it so that it can be a work of power and freedom in your life by filling up those empty places caused by negative influences.

Jesus was on a mission for humanity when He walked the earth. He came for the very purpose of setting people free. He desires you to be free!

Acts 10:38 states that "Jesus went about doing good and healing ALL that were oppressed by the Devil, because God was with him."

Again, the very name, Devil, is interpreted as the arch-enemy of good. The Bible also says in **Hebrews 13:8,** "Jesus is the same yesterday, today and forever."

Jesus' Mission is the same for you today as it was when He walked the earth!

So that you will realize that these things that happen to people are not coincidental but are the works of Satan, the arch-enemy of good, let's look at the height, depth, length and breadth of what oppression is and the form it can take in individuals' lives.

Chapter 9
Oppression versus Love

JESUS CAME TO DO GOOD AND TO SET YOU FREE FROM OPPRESSION!

If Jesus said He came for the purpose of relieving people of this oppression and healing them, we need to realize more fully what this covers! We will find that oppression takes on a completely different character than what the Bible says God's love is which Jesus came to proclaim to you and all mankind. The key to you being made complete (whole) with all the fullness of life God has in store for you is allowing Jesus to destroy (undo) the works (oppressive activity) of the devil that have held you captive.

In fact, it is so important for you to realize how much you are loved that the Apostle Paul says in **Ephesians 3:15-19** (New Living Translation)

"When I think of all this, I fall to my knees and pray to the Father, the Creator of everything in heaven and on earth. I pray that from his glorious, unlimited resources he will empower you with inner strength through his Spirit. Then Christ will make his home in your hearts as you trust in him. Your roots will grow down into God's love and keep you strong. And may you have the power to understand, as God's people should, how wide, how long, how high, and how deep his love is. May you experience the love of Christ, though it is too great to understand fully. Then you will be made complete with all the fullness of life and power that comes from God."

THIS TRUTH IS SO POWERFUL THAT THE APOSTLE PAUL SAID, "I FALL ON MY KNEES AND ASK GOD TO SHOW YOU THIS TRUTH ABOUT GOD'S LOVE AND THE UNLIMITED RESOURCES AVAILABLE TO YOU THE MORE YOU UNDERSTAND AND APPLY THESE TRUTHS TO YOUR LIFE!

This Scripture indicates that you becoming aware of how much you are loved is very high on God's agenda and will be the catalyst for you to experience "fullness of life."

JESUS SAID OPPRESSION IS NOT FROM HEAVEN!

Oppression, Jesus said, is Satan or the Devil's activity in our lives. Some of the meanings of oppression and how it manifests in peoples' lives are as follows:

"It," oppression, OR Satan's "behind the scene activity," exercises dominion against; keeps in subservience; governs or treats harshly; tyrannizes; makes tired; disheartens; discourages; is cruel; represses; afflicts; harasses; suffocates; weighs down with cares; overwhelms; burdens; troubles; abuses; persecutes by laying blame for a fault as well as encourages malicious talk in a way that damages a person's reputation.

THINK ABOUT HOW MANY WAYS YOU HAVE BEEN THE OBJECT OF OPPRESSIVE ACTIVITY? THIS ACTIVITY BEGINS IN THE THOUGHT REALM FIRST TO CAUSE YOU TO ACCEPT FEAR AND INTIMIDATION RATHER THAN LOVE AND SAFETY. IT PLACES HEAVY BURDENS AROUND PEOPLES' LIVES.

DO ANY OF THESE ACTIONS REFLECT GOD'S LOVE FOR YOU OR CARE AND CONCERN?

This is why Jesus came to destroy and undo these activities that have oppressed and enveloped peoples' lives that have left them with feelings of "there is no way out." He came to show us the way out and paid the price for us to be out from under such continual afflictions. If individuals you know have been used by the Oppressor to afflict your life, know that Jesus came to set you free from the results of those actions!

In fact in **Genesis 1:26**, it says this: "Then God said, "Let us make man in Our image, according to Our likeness; let them have dominion...""

God said He wanted us to have dominion, not be dominated and oppressed. Therefore, we can see that oppressive issues had nothing to do with God's intention for man. God gave man dominion and authority and free choice and unfortunately, Adam and Eve made the wrong choice. That is why Jesus came, to undo (disintegrate, smash) the works of the Devil so that we could experience the life He intended for Adam and Eve to live.

Do you need your thought life and your words about who you are changed so that you think, say and do in accordance with what God's desires are for you? Do you have walls around your mind about who you are that need to be smashed, disintegrated and undone so that you can have a mighty breakthrough in your thought life and circumstances?

ARE YOU READY TO GET YOUR MIND RECONDITIONED?

Are you tired of negative thought patterns controlling and dictating your life? As you condition yourself to learn the truth, you will become more free each day to live the abundant, joy-filled life God intends instead of living oppressed and weak. By applying these truths today and uprooting negative issues that have controlled you, your tomorrow will be so much better. When you "come into the knowledge of the truth," it does not take God long to do something big because you will truly have faith that there are good things in store for you!

Remember again one of the meanings of Satan's name is: "to plot against." He works diligently to make people think God does not have their best interest at heart! Isn't that how it all began? Satan accused God to Eve by suggesting to her that God did not have her best interest at heart and she fell for his lies. He still uses the same method of operating by suggesting to us that what God has promised in His Word cannot be really counted on.

ARE YOU AWARE OF WHERE THE THOUGHTS YOU ARE ACTING ON ARE COMING FROM?

Being aware of where your thoughts are coming from and having knowledge of God's Word will enable you to make right decisions and correct any areas where you have been thrown off course!

Jesus said in **John 10:10**, "The thief (Satan) has come but for to steal, kill and destroy. I have come that you might have life and have it more abundantly."

LET'S LOOK AT SATAN'S GOALS:
TO STEAL, TO KILL, TO DESTROY

NOW, LET'S LOOK AT THE GOALS OF OUR LORD JESUS CHRIST FOR YOU: ... "THAT YOU MIGHT HAVE LIFE AND THAT YOU MIGHT HAVE IT MORE ABUNDANTLY."

Unfortunately, if you tell some people God wants them abundantly blessed, they will get indignant and say, "If that is so, why are there so many bad issues in the world?"

The answer, I believe, begins when you can accept the truth about what Jesus said in **John 14:6**, "I am the Way, the Truth, and the Life," Please note, He did not say "I am one of many ways, or I am a truth, and I am a way of life. He made it very clear that He is the Answer.

He gave us the power to be Overcomers in this life. Obviously, an Overcomer has something he or she must overcome! He bought and paid for us to have the right to stand up against the forces that oppose God's desire for us. But! You have to be aware of who you are in Christ and you find this out through seeking Him through the Word of God and prayer. If you do not, you will fall for the deceptive lies Satan plants in your mind and act on them instead of the truth about how much God cares for you.

Hosea 4:6 says, "My people are destroyed because of lack of knowledge."

Please note, it does not say because of lack of God's love or willingness to do something for you. It says "lack of knowledge" of what He has in store for you when you find out the truth!

He also said in **John 14:9**, "If you have seen Me, you have seen the Father."

If you want to know what God is like, read the New Testament and notice how Jesus dealt with people. Jesus demonstrated the Father's love everywhere He went by "undoing" the works of the Devil, who was planting lies in peoples' lives and circumstances. One of the purposes for this book is to help you get to know experientially who Jesus is in you and for you to learn more about who you are in Him! That is what becoming born-again does! Being born-again restores your spirit-man back to the Father. Then, the goal of your faith is to restore your soul, which includes your mind, will and emo tions. You are on a search and find mission to find out and live out who He really created you to be; then you can help others find out the truth about who they were created to be! Whose report have you believed? Whose report are you living out today?

Chapter 10
Knowledge is power...but only if you use it!

THE OPPRESSOR WANTS YOU TO STAY IGNORANT OF GOD'S GOODNESS!

You have the choice but it does take time to study the Bible to find out what your inheritance as a child of God is. To compare it to something easily understood, suppose someone died and left a Will which included you as an inheritor and this act had the potential to enhance your life both emotionally and financially and you were either not aware of this Will or did not take the time to read it to find out what was yours. You would be missing out on the awareness of the love and respect that person had shown you by including you in their Will and the material benefits as well. It would have been there for you, but through lack of knowledge of it, you would have forfeited it. Jesus left us His Will. It is the New Testament!

Satan's method of operating has been to obscure the truth of how much God loves you and to intimidate you into thinking you have no rights, privileges or purpose as a child of God. It is vital that you realize that because you have been created to bring glory to God, you are a target of Satan who shoots his fiery darts (oppressive activity) to keep you and your loved ones in these negative oppressive habit patterns!

YOU DO HAVE A CHOICE BUT ONLY YOU CAN MAKE IT!

The problem is many people do not realize they have been given a choice and a way to get free. Many believe that "it is just the way it is" and there is no way out! By the time you finish reading and digesting this book, I believe you will realize you have powerful choices and will begin to make them!

The Bible speaks of Satan as the god of this world and the prince of the power of the air. As you know, a prince in the natural realm has an earthly kingdom that he rules over and so does Satan. Because of the authority given to him by Adam and Eve, he has used his rule working through individuals who were not properly connected to the love of God to cause painful circumstances which has altered who we really were created to be. This has left many of us with unhealed and unresolved issues in our emotional and feeling realm and our minds have become polluted!

WHAT IS YOUR MIND FULL OF?

To make it plain, our souls are full of lies, junk and misinformation that need to be dealt with if we are to live out the purpose Jesus offers us. We have to get rid of the results of oppressive thought patterns that lead to defeating actions in our life.

Again, not only have I experienced years of turmoil because of issues that have sought to define who I am, but countless others I have spoken to, ministered to and listened to have multiplied issues that have been passed on in the form of generational lies, ungodly belief systems and worldly pressures that have caused strongholds to be built around the individuals' minds. This has caused much suffering and hurting which God, through Jesus Christ, has provided redemption for.

There is a way to freedom! The way to get free is to learn and experience God's true heart of love and pull up bitter roots and strongholds by allowing Jesus, by the Holy Spirit, to show you areas of your life you need to revisit where you are being held captive. Most people are unaware of the significance these issues are having on them personally and need to learn progressively through the Word of God, (God's Manufacturer's Handbook) and revelations from the Lord that will help get them "unstuck" and free so they can experience the life God intended for them.

YOU DO NOT KNOW HOW MUCH YOU ARE IN BONDAGE TO UNTIL YOU GET FREE!

I can tell you from personal experience, you do not know how much you are in bondage to until you get free. I know what it is like to grow up in the middle of chaos, to make major mistakes in my personal life and to live life feeling ashamed, confused and rejected even though I knew that Jesus loved me and my mistakes were forgiven. I had to take time to revisit issues and oppressive feelings that were problematic for me over and over again. I had to get to the root of my feelings and issues and then release them to the Lord.

I encourage everyone that they should take time to get to the root of

35

their problems and then do what the Bible says to do: "Cast the whole [not part] of your cares on Him because He cares for you!" – **1 Peter 5:7**. The true meaning of "to cast" is to hurl away from you! Jesus does not want you carrying the weight and cares of yesterday. The burden gets much too heavy especially when He has already paid the price for your liberty. Unless you get rid of the cares and pain you are carrying, these become accumulative and will show up somewhere in your life in a negative way.

ARE YOU TIRED OF BEING CONFORMED? GET READY THEN TO BE TRANSFORMED!

Until you take time to get rid of emotional bondage which includes oppressive thought patterns and strongholds that have deep roots in your way of thinking and acting, you will live far beneath what God had in mind for you...you will be living a "conformed" life instead of a "transformed" life.

Jesus said in **John 8:32**, "If you continue in my Word you will know the truth and the truth will set you free." To "know" in this Scripture actually means "to experience." We all need an ongoing experience with continuing to learn God's truths about us to replace what we have accepted from others as the "gospel."

Another case in point is a lady who was shown that she was still carrying around with her the earliest memories and experiences she had as a little girl which was full of fear and subsequent insecurities. During the time the Lord was bringing these memories to her mind He showed her this was not what He wanted for her life. She was able to address those early fears and insecurities and make the decision to leave them behind and move on, and as she said,—to grow up! Since realizing what had been holding her back, she has felt a growing confidence and maturity that she hadn't realized before was hers by right even though she had been a Christian for many years. She said that from time to time the feelings try to creep back into her life but now she knows the truth and how to resist them in Christ Jesus!

Let's look at a powerful thought in **Psalms 51** which is speaking about the Lord when the Psalmist says: "Behold You desire truth in the inner being: make me therefore to know wisdom in my inmost heart or thoughts."

You see, that is exactly what Jesus did for this lady, He desired her to know the truth in her inmost thoughts so that she could be free from her past hurts and experiences and experience what He had for her in the here and now! It was wisdom from God that released that information and brought understanding to her.

God is pleased when you know His truth in your inner man and that is what you act on! If you do not have His truth stored in your heart, you will act on lies and experiences stored within you as we have described above. God's desires for you are like hidden treasures that you have to go digging for by spending time with Him and in His Word!

Chapter 11
The Word of God is an internal mirror!

THE WORD OF GOD IS ALIVE AND POWERFUL AND SO SIGNIFICANT IF WE ARE TO EXPERIENCE GOD'S BEST!

Hebrews 4:12 is a powerful truth that you need to realize in order to live an overcoming life! It says, "For the Word of God is alive and powerful. It is sharper than the sharpest two-edged sword, cutting between soul and spirit, between joint and marrow. It exposes our innermost thoughts and desires."

The Word is alive and its purpose is to help you think about yourself as God thinks about you so that you can do what God says you can do.

If you often feel left out, unworthy, unappreciated, etc., you must realize first that you are not an accident. You are here because it is God's intention for you to be on the earth. One of the definitions for the word "think" is to compute. If you would just take the time to "compute" your thoughts as they rise up by being aware of whether it is an uplifting "God thought" or a downcast "oppressive Satan thought" your life and how you feel could be changed dramatically.

As you will see from the following Scripture, you are not just a number! You are a very important person.

Psalms 139: 13-18, "For You formed my inward parts; you wove me in my mother's womb. I will praise you for I am fearful and wonderfully made; marvelous are your works, and that my soul knows very well!"

GOD THINKS YOU ARE WONDERFUL BECAUSE YOU ARE HIS CREATION!

What does your soul think about you? Stored negative emotions and what you think and say about yourself can cause self-sabotage which promotes feelings of inadequacy that will hinder you-- spiritually, physically, mentally, socially and financially! This has all been a part of Satan's plot to get you to think less of yourself when you were made in the image of God. You were created to reflect the Lord! You were created to "mirror" Him. He wants His words to be alive in you directing how you feel about yourself; not what others have said or down line ancestral issues! I continue to speak of this fact because, as we have studied, to the degree that you accept God's truths as opposed to your experiences and acceptance of the words of others, is the degree that you will live life and live it more abundantly.

Seeds that cause self-sabotage and poor self-image began in most peoples' lives when they were growing up. If you grew up in a discontented environment, that discontentment will continue to be experienced in some form in your life such as disharmony in family relationships, social and business situations and often some type of physical infirmity. The root causes or seeds which are entangled in negative mindsets and repressed feelings will find their way to surface sooner or later unless they are acknowledged and properly dealt with. Could you be someone experiencing some or all of these conflicts?

TO GET FREE, YOU MUST ACKNOWLEDGE WHAT IS GOING ON INSIDE OF YOU!

You need to ask Jesus to show you the roots of negative emotions and lies you believe about God, yourself and others so that this emotional baggage can be released to Jesus and those wounded places can then be filled with the truth of who you are today!

I am reminded of another lady who had such a low self-esteem problem and seemed to always look very sad. She took time to ask the Lord what the root cause of her feelings was and He showed her it stemmed from a time when as a little girl she so wanted to do ballet but her mother was unable to afford the fee for the classes. As a result, she would sit at the back of the hall during dress rehearsal while the other girls were dancing and having such a wonderful time. As she grew up she never had gotten past that little girl's hurt and embarrassment she felt until she had a vision of the Lord she describes as follows: She said Jesus took her out onto a huge stage, the same as when she was a little girl, and she danced in a stunning white and silver dress. The auditorium was packed and the people were applauding and Jesus was smiling and clapping behind the curtain! She said Jesus took that little girl that had the opportunity to experience how good it felt to be praised and appreciated and brought her to join her as an adult. From that time on, she has been healed from the hurt she had carried so long! Not only that, a sales colleague said to her, "We don't know what has happened to you, but you are a completely different person." She went from feeling like "the odd person out" to feeling part of a wonderful team!

Now I could have told her as an adult that she just needed to get over the embarrassment and hurt she felt as a child since she was now grown up. However, that would not have removed the wounds she had carried for so many years. She needed an experience with the One that loved her from the beginning and created her to enjoy good things.

Ephesians 4:23 says "We are to be renewed in the spirit of our mind." The Amplified translation says, "We are to be CONSTANTLY renewed."

It is a process, but the results are well worth the effort! Just as our physical body has been created with systems that release toxins on a daily basis, our emotional system in our soul needs to have toxic thoughts and experiences released so that each day can begin with healthy feelings and thoughts. So many people, because of lack of knowledge of the powerful influence it has, neglect the emotional area of life and consequently the ill-effects continue to build in their life and relationships as had happened in the aforementioned testimonies....until Jesus was given the opportunity to bring the truth they needed and then to heal their wounded emotions.

Psalms 139 continues: "My frame was not hidden from you when I was being formed in secret and intricately and curiously wrought as if embroidered with various colors in the depths of the earth..."

You are a magnificent God created specimen! Scientist, Dr. Carl Baugh, stated that our body is made up of 100 trillion cells that if they were stretched out would reach further than Mars! That is how intricate you are and specifically designed by God with intimate care! You are a very important person.....purpose made with love, creativity and care.

The Scripture continues, "Your eyes saw my unformed substance and in Your book all the days of my life were written before ever they took shape, when as yet there was none of them."

You are not an accident! You are so important to the Lord that He wrote a book about your life personally....imagine the Author of Life authoring a book about your life that He desires you to experience.

40

You were planned by the Lord to be here on this earth to receive His love and to enjoy the love and gifts He has placed within you. You were made in His image for a purpose.

JESUS BOUGHT BACK HIS ORIGINAL INTENTION FOR YOU!

When Jesus died on the cross and arose again, your true purpose in Christ was bought back so that you could have the opportunity to experience His original intention and design for you...not the world's pattern given you by ancestral situations, ungodly belief systems, and lack of knowledge of how important you are to God.

It is very much like this. My car has a system on it that allows me to set it the way I like: Lights on and off, steering setting, mirror settings, etc. One time I pressed a button which said, "Do you want the system to go back to the Manufacturer's Settings?" When we are born again, our lives are reset to our Manufacturer's Settings! He has set within us everything to work to the highest standard and the best purpose we were created for.

Maybe your purpose is to be a Chemical Engineer, a Teacher, an Evangelist, an Artist, an Architect, an Accountant, an Administrator, a Homemaker, a Volunteer, a Therapist, a Salesperson, a Waiter, etc. You will be able to move forward in your purpose when you remove negative hindering thought patterns about who you really are. When you get rid of negative, oppressive feelings and feelings accumulated through the years of trying to live up to others standards, you will then be in a better position to press forward in the life you were created to enjoy.

Also, another comparison is like the information that flashes in your car when you need an oil change or perhaps some part of the engine is overheating. It is there to let you know something needs to be looked at before something major happens to your car. When we have the same difficult issues over and over again we should be aware that these are flashing signs that something is not right! A correction needs to be made in our life and thinking processes so that our life will run more smoothly!

If you are not convinced as yet that there is a perfect will for your life and how important it is to the Lord that you realize and fulfill it, read on:

41

Psalms 139: 17 says: "How precious and weighty also are your thoughts TO ME, O God!"

In order to get a powerful picture of just what the Lord is saying to us, let's break down what some of the words in this Scripture actually mean:

PRECIOUS means: of great price, great worth and valuable! He is sending thoughts to you right now of what great worth you are to Him!

WEIGHTY means: momentous, important, and deserving of consideration!

God thinks you are special and worthy of consideration!

Verse 17 says God is sending all of these thoughts TO YOU. You have to believe this is true about you specifically to receive the benefits of these thoughts! I would encourage you to meditate on this powerful truth so that it can enhance your life. Remember the "walls" we spoke of earlier that surround our minds and disposition, they must come down so that the truth of who you are can come in. If your life experiences have taught you something different, you should take time to really feel the depth of this truth.

If a feeling or a thought that God does not love you or care about you seems to be blocking you being able to accept how much you are loved, take a few minutes to ask Jesus to show you where this feeling began so that you can remove the blockage by giving the memory or memories to Him. The block could have come from a painful situation that happened to you or even misinformation that you believed to be true, but was not! Thoughts are things and unless you let go of "things" they are still with you and you will act on them on a subconscious level.

Opening the "door" to your heart will enable you to receive all of these valuable, wonderful thoughts God is sending your way on a daily basis. Just as it is important that you receive and act on God's thoughts to you, it is vital that you do not dwell on negative thoughts you may be picking up from people around. You can easily tell the difference! One will promote a sense of truth and well being and the other will cause you to feel fearful and/or self-conscious. God wants you to know from Him who you really are!

Chapter 12
What are your thoughts telling you today?

REMEMBER: THOUGHTS ARE THINGS. RECEIVE THE "THINGS" GOD IS SENDING TO YOU TODAY!

Remember how important it is for you to "compute" your thoughts! His thoughts would be for your joy, love, contentment, health, success, empowerment to fulfill the desires of your heart! Yes, that is a promise as well. **Psalms 37:4** says "Delight thyself in the Lord and He will give you the desires of your heart!"

It brings a thought to my mind of how often I have been talking with someone yet I knew their thoughts were far off and their attention was not on what I was saying. How often are we that way with the Lord? Yet think of how much more empowered we would be to experience life if we would become aware with our whole heart and mind of His true intentions for us on a daily basis.

Psalms 139:17 goes on to say about God's thoughts coming to us: "How vast is the sum of them,"

VAST means – immense, huge, and very great!

Think about huge and great and vast thoughts from the King of Kings and Lord of Lords coming to you now!

The verse continues: "If I could count them, they would be more in number than the sand of the sea."

What an awesome thought! Try to picture counting the sand of the sea! It is impossible. However God uses that analogy to get you to realize how important you are to Him. Again, why not reach out in faith and grab God's thoughts of how precious, how valuable, how immense, huge and of very great importance you are to Him today, that He would give you that much thought! Make a conscious effort to do this until it becomes reality in your life. He wants you to realize that you are important to Him! God's word says "His words are life to those that find them and healing to all their flesh!" **Proverbs 4:22.**

THINK ABOUT THIS!

If you are not receiving God's thoughts, you are forfeiting blessings and life experiences that He has planned for you.

God's Word says that people perish for two reasons:

1. Lack of knowledge [which is not knowing the truths of God], **Hosea 4:6**, and
2. No vision: no dream or something to look upon with contentment! **Proverbs 29:18**.

God has dreams for you to be the "HEAD" and not the "TAIL" according to **Deuteronomy 28:13**. Take a moment to feel that truth in your current circumstances. Picture, which means to have a vision, what you would be doing if you knew that were really true, because it is!

Proverbs 23:7 SAYS, "AS A MAN THINKS (COMPUTES) IN HIS HEART, SO IS HE."

WHEN THE BIBLE SPEAKS OF THE HEART, DO YOU KNOW WHAT THAT MEANS?

What you think in your "heart" which literally includes your thoughts, your awareness, your feelings, your perceptions or your center is what will dictate your life whether it is true or not! Perception comes through your feelings and senses and is usually based on your experiential past. Therefore, if you perceive something to be true in your heart, whether it is correct or not, you will act on it as though it were true.

This is exactly what **Proverbs 23:7** means: As (YOU) think [compute] in your heart so are you. It is important that you understand, therefore, how you think about yourself is a big key to your success and enjoyment of life.

GOD WANTS YOUR LIFE TOUCHED WITH HIS TRUTH!

All through the New Testament, the Lord seeks to make us aware of the height, the depth, the length and breadth of His love. He wants every area of our lives and circumstances touched with His love and truth because He desires us to excel in being who He created us to be. What I am seeking to challenge you with in this book is to become more aware of your thoughts. Do they impact you with a sense of well-being or do they make you feel oppressed? Where are they coming from!

This is where "the rubber meets the road" so to speak. **Isaiah 53** says: "WHO'S REPORT WILL YOU BELIEVE?" Look at your life. Whose report have you believed?

God wants you to rely on His love. **1 John 4: 15 & 16**, "If anyone acknowledges that Jesus is the Son of God, God lives in him and he in God. And so we know and rely on the love God has for us. God is love. Whoever lives in love lives in God and God lives in him."

It is important, as this Scripture says, that "we RELY on the love God has for us." We could also say that we need to "trust" in the love God has for us. I know for so many years even after I was born again, I was so afraid of displeasing the Lord. I was fearful of making mistakes because I grew up in an environment where unconditional love was not part of my life's experience. I transferred this fear into my relationship with the Lord and others. Therefore, instead of experiencing freedom, I became fearful that I would do or say something that offended God or someone and I seemed to always feel pressured and guilty.

I needed to learn more from the Word of God and to experience more of His Presence in my life so that I could feel safe and secure in His love for me as my Father. I needed to "rely" on His love because He said I should! I was not able to experience the abundant, successful, enjoyable, fruitful life the Bible speaks about, and that Jesus said He came to earth to give, because I was full of the painful experiences and negative thought patterns of yesterday and I lacked the true knowledge of my Heavenly Father's love. It seemed I kept making the same mistakes over and over again. I did not know how to rely on God's unconditional love. What about you?

DO YOU LACK THE TRUE KNOWLEDGE OF YOUR HEAVENLY FATHER'S LOVE? AFTER ALL, HE DID ADOPT YOU INTO HIS FAMILY!

Do you feel loved unconditionally or do you feel you have to "work" to have God's love and the acceptance of others to feel good about yourself?

To get further insight into how our lives can get stuck and off course, let me share a story I read that happened in Seattle:

The City Development Committee decided to take a large area that had been the city dump and to use the land to develop a beautiful park where people could read, exercise, eat, play, bring their families; a place of beauty and enjoyment. So the land was leveled, and it became just that.

However, after some time the garbage underneath the ground began to emit sickening gases and poisonous vapors and it became so bad that the park, created to be a place of beauty and enjoyment, now was no longer useful. It had to be closed!

Had the poisonous effects of years of junk and garbage being dumped in this landfill been properly dealt with in the beginning, this would not have happened.

Our lives are very much like that. Again, I want to point out the powerful impact of getting rid of wrong thinking (mind pollution) as presented in **Romans 12:1**. The Apostle Paul literally begs, appeals, requests earnestly, beseeches and implores us TO DEAL WITH THE HIDDEN THINGS IN OUR LIVES, which is the subconscious experiential area of our minds that we act on without realizing it...the world pattern set in us from birth.

Let's go over this Scripture again from the Amplified Bible. It says: "I appeal to you therefore brethren and beg of you in view of ALL the mercies of God that you make a dedication of your bodies as a living sacrifice, holy and well pleasing to God which is your spiritual service of worship. Do not be conformed to the pattern of the world, but be transformed by the renewing of your mind so that you can prove what is the good, acceptable and perfect will of God for you in Christ Jesus:"

If we are not careful, we will read over the mercies of God without realizing the impact of the truth being set forth here. This alone can so change a person's thoughts about how important they are to God thereby redirecting their entire life in a powerful way.

The Mercy spoken of in this Scripture actually means: His PITY towards us, His COMPASSION, His FAVOR and a word picture of Him BENDING OR STOOPING IN KINDNESS TOWARDS US!

Chapter 13
Time for a fresh new mental attitude?

"WOW," IS THAT A DIFFERENT PICTURE THAN YOU HAVE HAD OF GOD BEFORE?

That is a lot different than an angry God who is just sitting in heaven waiting for us to make another mistake so He can give us a thrashing! Is that the way you would treat your children that you love so much? Watching and waiting for them to make a mistake so that you could tell them how terrible they are?

God wants our minds delivered from the superficial customs of the world and changed and revolutionized entirely by acknowledging and experiencing who we are in Christ Jesus...He wants us to get a fresh new mental attitude! God wants you to think about yourself as He does. When we begin to think of ourselves as important to God who wants us to experience His best, our actions will line up with that truth. Our lives will begin to become fruitful and enjoyable. This will bring Him much joy and praise.

Jesus said in **John 14:30**, "The evil genius or prince or ruler of this world is coming and he has found nothing in me?" Jesus knew that Satan, or the prince of this world, was always looking for an open door or weak place to get a stronghold. Remember, Jesus came to earth to be our example...to show us the way to live victoriously.

Prayerfully, the time you take to uproot and remove "stuff" sent by the "evil genius" will put you in a position to say, as Jesus did, "he has found nothing in me!"

Living a fear based life causes us to have weak places in our emotions that causes us to live stress-filled lives which depresses and hinders our immune system. We not only get spiritually locked up, but physically and mentally as well. According to Dr. Candace Pert, author of "Molecules of Emotion," unexpressed or repressed emotions end up locked up in the body causing various physical ailments. Just like the park in Seattle, emotions that have not been dealt with will surface in a negative way spoiling our life in one way or another unless they are dealt with.

WHAT IS YOUR BODY TELLING YOU ABOUT YOUR EMOTIONAL STATE?

A case in point is this: There was a lady in England that my husband and I ministered to. She was struggling with severe arthritis in her hands, in fact, her hands were totally twisted, and she could only walk a little distance and had a debilitating problem with her eyes as well which required her to wear dark glasses all of the time. During a time of prayer ministry to her, the Lord revealed a lie she had believed about her parents since she was a little girl that had caused her to feel severe rejection, hopeless, ashamed and unwanted. She had misinterpreted a situation and had stored up anger towards her parents for years. Once she realized the truth and let these painful twisted memories go, her body began to relax and she began physical restoration!

When we have repressed feelings brought on by pressures of life and the sense of hopelessness that can surround these feelings, we begin to judge, condemn and criticize others as well as put ourselves down. Strife in our hearts leads to confusion and can open the door to every evil work (**James 3:16**) physically, mentally, spiritually and socially.

WE NEED TO CLEANSE OUR EMOTIONAL MEMORY BANK!

The result of this is that very often we get frustrated and not only reject God's love, but we also reject the love and friendship of those around us who may not have had anything to do with the original hurt and wounds at all. Again **Proverbs 23:7** says, "As a man thinks in his heart, so is he." You can easily see why Satan has been so busy endeavoring to get us to think wrong thoughts towards God, our families, friends and ourselves. This causes our lives to get all twisted.

We need to get back to believing God's report about who we are. To do this we must let go of the "things" that have become issues which have held us captive as was the case with the woman from England. She began her restoration process by unlocking her emotional memory bank. Just getting rid of that one lie changed her image of who she was and her body began adapting to the new sense of well being.

I read of a doctor who said that every emotion you have ever experienced whether good or bad is stored somewhere in your body. Do you need an emotional memory house cleaning? I sure did and I still am a work in progress!

This next Scripture reveals in another dramatic way why it is so vital to be aware of what we are thinking and its effects on our life and circumstances.

ARE YOU MISSING THE GRACE OF GOD?

Hebrews 12:15 "See to it that no one misses the grace of God and that no bitter root grows in measure to cause trouble and defile many." The Amplified translation says to "Exercise foresight and be on the watch to look [after one another] to see that no one falls back from and fails to secure God's grace (His unmerited favor and spiritual blessing) in order that NO root of resentment (rancor, bitterness or hatred) shoot forth and cause trouble or bitter torment and many become contaminated and defiled by it."

Case in point: That one precious lady from England had a bitter root that defiled her life for many years.

Are you carrying around misconceptions as this lady did? Is there someone in your life you need to forgive? The true meaning of forgive is to release! Do you need to release others as well as yourself? I conscientiously do this on a regular basis GOD DOES NOT WANT US TO MISS HIS GRACE, HIS LOVE AND KINDNESS because He knows what the results of negative thoughts and failure to release yourself and others with true forgiveness will be in your life.

But He says to us this is an area that "WE" must see to it so that we do not miss out on all He has planned. We must pull up the bitter or poisonous roots that have caused our lives to become defiled. Defile means to make dirty, pollute, corrupt, desecrate, and poison! In other words, bitter roots will stop you from being your best.

Also, when there is pain in our lives that has not been acknowledged and dealt with, we will seek "counterfeit" love to comfort us through

EXCESSES in life and an overpowering need for acceptance and approval by others etc.. We look for anything to fill the void in us caused by unhealed bitter roots. This then can be the reason for an ongoing cycle of painful and destructive events and defeats.

We can readily understand why the Lord urges us to take care of these issues. We know that if God requires something of us, He is there to help us. We need revelation, which means revealed light, from the Lord as to what our specific bitter roots are, where these bitter roots began and we need to systematically release them from within so that we will no longer be stuck or hindered. So many of the "case in point" testimonies show how true this is and vital so that you can live in the NOW without being controlled and inhibited by your past!

Chapter 14
Pull out the bitter roots

UNLESS YOU KNOW WHAT A BITTER ROOT IS,
YOU WILL NOT BE ABLE TO UPROOT IT AND
GET RID OF IT...ONCE AND FOR ALL!

Perhaps a little more insight into how bitter roots change us would be helpful because these will always alter our perception of God and others. Let's take time to learn more about what a bitter root is so that it can be exposed and rooted out so that healing can begin.

According to the Greek definition, a bitter root is a poison (a negative thought pattern) that manifests itself in the following ways:

It soils our life and relationships; it tarnishes (as silver); it taints or infects even with disease; it diminishes the purity of the splendor God created for our life; it actually means to become sully or sullen which causes us to have these personality traits: passive, resentful, unforgiving, gloomy, unsociable - not responsive to friendliness or encouragement or urging; stubbornly ill-humored, morose, dismal – all which lead to ill temper and depression.

ISN'T IT TIME WE GET RID OF THE EFFECTS OF BITTER ROOTS SO THAT WE CAN REFLECT THE GLORY OF GOD INSIDE AND OUT?

Depression is known as one of the leading causes of physical sickness, and depression is often described as anger turned inward. According to Dr. Candace Pert in "Molecules of Emotion," depression takes the following progression: depression, anger, sadness and the root is fear. So when we have bitter roots, we put walls around our lives that not only keep God and His love out but keeps people and opportunities out as well.

Take time to take an inventory of your life. Does the description of how bitter roots can affect us describe you? If so, now is the time to make a decision to get rid of these issues so your life can move forward with the blessings God has in store for you.

Here are some other issues in the form of "word curses" that can be a source for developing bitter roots in your soul. If you as a child or an adult have heard put downs such as these:

"You are no good."
"No one will ever want you."
"You can't do anything right."
"No one is interested in you."
"All you are is trouble."
"You were born on the wrong side of the tracks."
"You will never get a better job or be able to do such and such."
"You are stupid."
"You are too fat."
"You are ugly."

These are words that build bitter roots in your emotions of hopelessness, feelings of aloneness and abandonment, self-rejection, mistrust, poor self-image and promote feelings of being trapped with no way out. Again, because of this, many seek consolation and comfort through excesses in food, drugs, counterfeit love relationships, etc., all which block us from receiving God's love and the love of others he wants to send our way.

If you think about what we have learned so far about the importance of realizing the truth about what God says about us, you can see that none of the above statements are the truth. They may be what you have experienced; however, you are never "too" anything because "With God all things are possible" according to **Matthew 19:26**!

Unless we deal with these lies and wrong thought patterns (or world thought patterns) and reject and renounce these, we will be set up for failure in life by the oppressor...not God! Wrong thoughts set up boundaries that limit our receiving all of God's blessings that have already been provided through knowledge of Jesus Christ and who He created us to be! Acceptance of negative words about who you are will definitely block and hinder the truth about who you were created to be.

YOU NEED TO BECOME THE DOORKEEPER TO YOUR HEART!

Proverbs 4:23 says "(You) keep your heart with all vigilance and above all that you guard, for out of it flow the springs/issues/boundaries of life."

Unless these words and their effect on how we think about ourselves are pulled out by the roots through revelation from the Word of God as well as the Holy Spirit, and replaced with the truth or right thoughts, individuals will literally forfeit the abundant joy-filled life Jesus came for them to experience.

HOW MANY PEOPLE DO YOU KNOW WHO ARE CALLED TO BETTER THINGS THAN THEY ARE CURRENTLY EXPERIENCING?

Again, that is why we are urged in such a dramatic way not to be conformed to the pattern the world has set for us. WE MUST see to it that NO bitter root takes hold of our lives and if there are some there, we must pull them out and begin planting the truth of how much we are loved by God and what great things He has in store for us WHO WILL BELIEVE!

Unfortunately, because people have not been aware of the poisonous effect of allowing these bitter roots to grow or even how they got there, so many are living far beneath what God's desires are for them. Are you one of them?

We must get the junk out! Otherwise it contaminates and spoils our faith and our lives. We walk around looking sad and tarnished when Jesus said in **John 17**, "That glory that You gave Me, I give to them!" That includes you and me! His glory is a precious gift we must receive to experience it. He definitely did not create you and pour Himself inside of you to have you going around sad, hopeless and defeated.

We are often told by people around us to "Just get over it!" To get over it, we must get to the root of the problem, the "it" and then we can move forward. You know that the Bible uses natural parallels to give us understanding of spiritual things. If you have a garden with beautiful flowers you are aware that you must keep the weeds out so that they will not choke the flowers. Unless the weeds are pulled out by the roots and not just nipped off at the top, the weeds soon return and spoil your garden.

Our lives are like that. The bitter roots that are allowed to grow soon choke out the truths for us in the Word of God that would cause us to bear fruit and have positive experiences in our lives.

In my book, "Power Thoughts for Triumphant Living," there is a story about a car that I was driving which accidentally had the wrong fuel put in that caused this wonderful high-powered automobile to completely shut down. It no longer performed as the Manufacturer had intended until the engine was flushed out and the right fuel was put back in! Our lives are the same. Without a revelation of God's love to us flooding our being, we do not live the life God's intends for us. Faith works by love. We can only give out what we have received. Has wrong fuel, negative words, thoughts and experiences been stopping your life from fulfilling God's intentions for you?

Chapter 15
Where did that come from?

WOULDN'T IT BE WONDERFUL TO EXPERIENCE THE LIFE GOD CREATED FOR YOU TO LIVE?

Truths from this book and revelations from the Lord can set you on your way to a much happier purpose filled life! You can begin to live the life God had in mind for you to live when He created you!

We need to allow Jesus to go to the different layers and levels of our pain where wrong information has been put in us and stored and allow healing to come one level at a time. Just as our cars need an oil change and tune up on a regular basis, our emotional memory bank needs this flushing out and tuning up so that we can live a fulfilled life in the here and now.

I want to encourage you to take time to ask the Lord to show you areas where the world and your life experiences have defined who you are instead of who God says you are.

HE WANTS TO DO THIS FOR YOU. EXPECT HIM TO BRING TO YOUR MIND WHAT YOU NEED TO KNOW SO THAT YOU CAN BE ON YOUR WAY TO BECOMING "FREE INDEED."

It is important to point out again that these could be negative experiences from early childhood or other relationships that have caused big issues to arise in your life today that involved your parents, husband, wife, friends, school mates, neighbors, business or ministry associates, etc. If you have accepted these negative experiences and allowed them to determine who you are over what God says, there will be a "pattern of the world" operating in your life that sets you up for brokenness, emotional damage, rejection, self rejection, feelings of unworthiness, lack of confidence and these are the mind sets we often act on instead of what the Lord has paid the price for us to experience.

These are bitter roots caused by mind pollution and they will cause defeat in your life because toxic emotions send chemical messages to your physical body that need to be released!

Hurt people hurt people! You must be willing to be willing to get rid of these hurts that have grown from bitter roots!

In fact, scientists say we react in 1000th of a second to our experiences instead of acting on the present situation. If you have stored negative experiences in your emotional memory bank, you will subconsciously react to the negative rather than the present moment which is exactly the activity the enemy has subtly set up! Have you ever been in a situation that you said something or reacted to someone and thought, "Why did I do that?" "Where did that come from?"

The good news is that when we deal with our negative emotional issues, we begin planting new experiences based on the present and who we are in Christ. Then our lives become fruitful just as the Lord had intended before Adam and Eve sinned in the garden. We are no longer giving any ground for the enemy to work in our lives to destroy current relationships whether family, business or whatever. The cause behind these negative cycles is cast out of our garden of life!

Have you ever thought about the fact that a lie is the opposite of the truth? Jesus wants you to know the truth about the lies that have been deposited in you, the lies that have taken up residence in your mind, will and emotions about whom you are!

Think again about what **III John** says, "BELOVED!!! I wish above all things that you would prosper and be in health even as your soul prospers!"

This Scripture is God's desire. Life is a journey. Many of us have been trying to build our lives on the Word but, like the park in Seattle, often we have been planting the Word of God on top of rubbish in the form of years of fears, doubts, failures, mistakes, disappointments, self judgments, and criticisms about who we are and BECAUSE OF THIS we are experiencing the same effect as the park, sooner or later the junk comes to the top and areas of our life whether in family situations, ministry, business, health, happiness get SHUT DOWN! Our soul needs cleaning out so that we can prosper and be in health and be able to enjoy our journey, which is a gift from God!

Chapter 16
What an amazing gift: Peace of mind and heart!

YOU HAVE A LOT OF INFORMATION STORED IN YOUR BRAIN THAT YOU ARE ACTING ON!

This Scripture indicates that our prosperity, which literally means – "success on your journey in life in family and in business" and our health are connected to our soul—As stated before, our soul is made up of the mind, the will and emotions. The mind is the storage room for every event in our lives. In fact, in the book, "Making the Most of Your Mind," it states that the complexity of the world's entire telephone systems is equivalent to a part of your brain the size of an ordinary garden pea. At any given moment there are between 100,000 and 1,000,000 chemical reactions taking place in your brain. It describes your brain as a biological supercomputer! Think of all the information stored in your brain right now that you are acting on!

Think again about the fact that when things happen or are said to us, the information based on our experiences that has been stored in our "supercomputer" is pulled from the emotional part of our brain in 1000th of a second or by the time you blink twice, you react based on stored information, instead of acting in the present!

It is important to point out **Proverbs 4:23** which says, "[You] Guard your heart for out of it comes the issues (boundaries) of life." Whatever is allowed into your heart, your feelings and intellect, is what can determine how far you get in life. Notice "You" is the understood subject in this verse. You must tend the garden of your heart and pull out the limiting thought patterns that are "setting boundaries" in your life and be aware that many of the "issues" and "thought patterns" were thrust on you from early childhood when you did not know how to deal with them properly. They still became a part of your memory bank and played a big part in the person you are today. As a comparison, on my computer it is often necessary to "defrag" it because too much information has been put in the wrong places. This has caused my computer to operate very slowly. Our minds are like that. We need to "defrag" our minds. We need to empty out bad, confusing memories and allow new information to come in that will bring about better experiences in life.

IT'S TIME TO TAKE THE TRASH OUT!

Knowing you are really loved unconditionally and created with personal intimate detail will help clean up the rubbish and drive fear and misconceptions out of your life! Just like you take the garbage in your house out to be taken to a dump, you must give the years, months and days of built up emotional garbage to Jesus so that it does not continue to "stink up" or pollute your mind and life!

I Corinthians 5:21, "For God made Christ who never sinned to be the offering for our sin so that we could be made right with God through Christ."

Jesus became sin for us so that we could become righteous before God. He did this for you and me. Right or Righteousness in this Scripture means: He has made us innocent. He justified us. We have equity of character. Equity also means investment. These are such powerful truths that can help you release feelings of shame, guilt, remorse and poor self image because Jesus bore (or took) these issues and the feelings contained in them so that you could experience being right with God.

God has a big investment in you! Because of His great love for you, His Son willingly gave His life as ransom for you. That is a big investment in you and the cost is beyond measure.

God does not want us to go around feeling like second-class citizens when we have been made citizens of Heaven.

Satan always wants us to feel condemned, guilty and rejected. He is the accuser. God, on the other hand convicts our hearts so that His truth can be exchanged for the lies Satan uses to accuse us, belittle us, and distort God's love and plan for our lives. Again, Satan, who is also known as the tormentor, subtly uses people to accomplish his negative purposes.

Our friend, the Holy Spirit is spoken of by Jesus as the Comforter. Comforter is quite different than tormentor, yet we often go around feeling unsettled, dreading "stuff" without really knowing where it is coming from! Now you can know.

AS A COMPARISON, THINK ABOUT HOW GOOD A FEATHER-FILLED COMFORTER FEELS ON A COLD DAY. JUST WRAPPING IT AROUND MAKES YOU FEEL WARM AND CONTENTED. OUR COMFORTER, THE HOLY SPIRIT, WANTS US TO 'FEEL' SETTLED AND SAFE AND WRAPPED IN HIS LOVE!

Being aware of your thoughts and feelings and where they are coming from will enable you to make a decision to accept or reject them before they become a part of you so that you will have success and not cycles of defeat in life.

God says in **Jeremiah 29:10**, "For I know the thoughts and plans that I have for you, thoughts and plans for welfare and peace and not for evil, to give you hope in your final outcome."

GOD KNOWS WHAT HIS THOUGHTS ARE TOWARDS YOU AND WANTS YOU TO KNOW AS WELL, AND.... THEY ARE GOOD AND NOT EVIL! KNOWING HIS THOUGHTS ARE FOR YOUR VICTORY WILL GIVE YOU CONFIDENCE WHEN THE PRESSURES OF LIFE MAKE YOU WANT TO GIVE UP BECAUSE YOU THINK NO ONE REALLY CARES ABOUT WHAT IS HAPPENING TO YOU.

John 14:27 in the Living Bible Jesus says: "I am leaving you with a gift—peace of mind and heart! And the peace I give isn't fragile like the peace the world gives. So don't be troubled or afraid."

What an amazing gift! Jesus is saying that our peace is so important that he deems it as a gift. If someone gave you a gift, you would have to open it and use it to reap the benefits of it.

YOU NEED TO KNOW HOW IMPORTANT THIS GIFT OF PEACE IS!

Have you opened and experienced this gift fully? According to the Greek Text, "Peace" means to be "set at one again" and "nothing missing, nothing broken," and "to have a prosperous journey!" God wants our relationship brought back to what He had intended before Adam and Eve fell...ONE WITH HIM. He wants each of us to have a Garden of Eden in fellowship with Him that He planned. He desires our lives to be joined back with Him so that we become complete in Him—literally nothing missing, nothing broken! This is the "gift of peace" Jesus is offering us. Peace is so much more than calmness, it is wholeness!

Chapter 17
Life and Death are in the power of the tongue

HAVE YOU LET PEOPLE AND CIRCUMSTANCES DICTATE WHAT YOU BECOME IN LIFE? HE WANTS TO HEAL YOUR BROKEN PLACES SO THAT YOU MAKE RIGHT CHOICES

The Bible says about Adam in **Gen. 2:7**, "God breathed into his nostrils the breath of life."

May I share with you something so very impacting? What that means is that God breathed into mankind (you), divine inspiration, intellect, a blast of himself and His passion!

The purpose for Jesus coming was to make His Father's love known and to enable us to experience this blast of Himself in our lives as He had intended for Adam.

In **John 17**, part of Jesus prayer is as follows: **v. 20-23** "I am praying not only for these disciples but also for all who will ever believe in me through their message. I pray that they will all be one just as you and I are one—as you are in me, FATHER, and I am in you. And may they be in us so that the world will believe you sent me. I have given them the glory you gave me, so they may be one as we are one. May they experience such perfect unity that the world will know that you sent me and that you love them as much as you love me."

Can you imagine what an important prayer this is and how important it is to realize what it means?

We know that this prayer was answered because Jesus said, "Father, I know you always hear Me!" **John 11:23**

He gave Himself for this very purpose so that you can experience the Father's love and walk in His glory which is a lot better than fear, worry and dread.

GOD'S DESIRES FOR YOU ARE A SAFE, HAPPY AND PROSPEROUS JOURNEY.

This is what this book is all about. Helping you to experience how much your Heavenly Father loves you and desires a safe, happy, prosperous journey for you. Becoming more aware of this and acting on it can change the course of your life.

THIS DOES NOT MEAN, OF COURSE, THAT YOUR LIFE WILL BE TROUBLE FREE, BECAUSE WE LIVE IN A FALLEN WORLD.

Jesus said, "In this world you will have tribulation, but be of good cheer for I have overcome the world." **John 16:33**

TRIBULATION HERE, AS RECORDED IN THE ORIGINAL GREEK TEXT, MEANS "ANYTHING THAT BURDENS THE SPIRIT," "AN AFFLICTION," "PERSECUTION," AND "ANGUISH" OR "A PRESSURING PRESSURE."

Needless to say, I am sure you who are reading this book either have or are in the midst of dealing with tribulation because the world we live in is full of it. However....this book has sought to point out how the adversary seeks to oppose God's purposes and plans through tribulation and oppression; BUT, knowledge of God's Word shows us how to triumph through Christ Jesus and to overcome with faith the circumstances that seek to control our lives.

When you go into a dark room and turn the light on, darkness leaves and you are able to see the obstacles in your path. His Word will bring light into your life so that you, too, can overcome obstacles that cause tribulation and block your peace!

II Corinthians 5:17, "If any man be in Christ, he is a new creature." (New Creature actually means brought back to the original formation of the Manufacturer!)

Earlier, we discussed how my car computer asked, "Do you want to go back to the Manufacturer's Settings?" Certainly, as born again creations, we want to get back to the original person God created us to be and get spirit-formed instead of situation/circumstance formed or as discussed earlier "conned and formed!" That is a good place to build from—our original purpose. We have the opportunity every day to re-author our lives based on the truth the Lord established for us.

We know from years of ministering to people that if their inner child, that is still a part of them psychologically, emotionally and spiritually has experienced trauma or if their inner child did not learn or experience healthy interpersonal skills, the adult can get "stuck" and unsure and scared in many situations that life presents because that inner child is still carrying the emotional scars which are being acted upon rather than acting as adults in the present moment! You have already read several testimonies of how this was absolutely true in these peoples' lives until Jesus brought them the truth and they became free from the "emotional scars" that had caused them to get stuck.

DO YOU STILL FEEL STUCK?

You can know you are stuck and need release if you have trouble functioning in every day life; if you keep experiencing a lack of success or feelings of well-being, if you carry feelings of unhappiness and/or an inability to identify and ask for what you really desire. Another issue that causes cycles of defeat (or getting stuck) is that many people are still carrying shame because of things they have done and things that have been done to them. These shameful experiences are stored in their emotional memories and they will continue to be acted on unless these are released.

A case in point is of a gentleman very active in church ministry who just seemed like a little child in a grown up body. After a time of ministry, the Holy Spirit revealed to him a time in early childhood that he had been mocked and made fun of and referred to as the character in a comic book who was a weakling and fearful and that is basically what he became. Because of this embarrassment and harassment, he was emotionally stuck as this little boy still carrying the wounds. Once he realized the stronghold this had on him for all of these years, even into adulthood, he released these feelings to the Lord and was, from that point on, the adult he desired to be.

ARE YOU LIVING YOUR LIFE AS A SURVIVOR RATHER THAN A VICTOR?

Another way many are carrying pain and are kept from experiencing life in its fullness is that most survivors teach their children survival and this survival mode is passed down. The survival mode often exhibits itself in angry words spoken to children such as: "You have made your bed, now go lay in it, etc." "I had to do such and such to get by, why shouldn't you?" These are negative words that will cause generations to continue going down a downhill slope unless the Lord is allowed into these painful situations to bring hope, healing and truth about His unconditional love and a higher purpose for their life.

It has been said that because we have made mistakes does not mean that we are a mistake; and just because we have had failures in our lives does not mean that we are a failure. So many people get locked into these errors in thinking and never receive the freedom offered by the Lord.

WE ALL NEED TO BE ENCOURAGED AND PRAISED.

Also, many people never received words of love and acceptance that would direct their lives in a positive way. They were filled with negative thought patterns to live out rather than the love God had intended with feelings of safety and security. Parental rejection is the worst pain anyone can experience in their emotional being!

Think about when you were a child how you were looked at, reprimanded and spoken to! Little children do not know how to deal with these things in their emotions if they have never experienced consistency in parental love. Again, this is in no way meant to demean these parents because often this was what they learned. It is, hopefully, going to change the way many people deal with their children so a new way of living will be experienced.

If these areas are not dealt with, they become self-defining which allows what others have said about you to define who you become.

DID YOU KNOW THAT THE TONGUE HAS GREAT POWER FOR GOOD OR EVIL?

The Bible says in **Proverbs 18:21**, "Life and death are in the power of the tongue." What life have you had spoken over your life by yourself or others. Equally as important, what defeat or criticisms have been spoken into or over your life? Life words carry hope and vitality so that you can fulfill your destiny and dreams. Negative words steal, kill and destroy and can hinder dramatically you being truly successful in life. Negative words and thoughts make life a struggle and can cause destructive thinking habits and life patterns that keep us away from the Father, His love and the love from others He sends our way.

This book is about opening your soul to the love of God. Receive His thoughts to you. Get rid of baggage in your thought life. God wants the tenderness of the Son of God to flow into you and out to others!!!

This will happen if you allow the Holy Spirit to show you areas in your emotions such as have been outlined above, that may be holding you captive (a prisoner of war) and remove them by releasing them. I can imagine as you have been reading this book you are realizing that some things that may have seemed little before have had a dramatic effect on your life and who you are today.

Healing wounded personalities was and is a big part of Jesus' ministry! Realize that lost years caused by negative words, thoughts, behavior can be redeemed and reversed. God wants your life to reflect His truth not what you have experienced!

Chapter 18
Lighten your load and unlock your burdens

DO YOU HAVE ANY IDEA OF WHAT BONDAGES YOU ARE CARRYING?

Interestingly enough, you do not know what you are in bondage to until you are free of it. My husband and I have seen people set free from the results of years of antagonism, frustration and put-downs who have begun a fresh life of joy and peace by allowing Jesus to show them where their pain began. Jesus wants to get behind the walls that have kept His love out.

WOULD YOU BE WILLING TO SET TIME ASIDE ON A REGULAR BASIS AND ALLOW THE LORD TO BRING RELEASE?

AGAIN, HERE ARE SIMPLE BUT POWERFUL STEPS THAT WE HAVE BEEN SHOWN BY THE LORD TO GET YOU SET FREE!
(See the **Life Shaping Prayer Method** in the back of this book)

If you are one of those individuals that are ready to get rid of your pain, now is the time to sit quietly in prayer and ask the Lord to show you where "it" (YOUR ISSUES) all began. The realization can come in the form of pictures of people or events, feelings, thoughts and impressions. As each memory comes, it is vital that you do not filter the memory out or say, "Oh that is just me." These memories are coming up so that you can gain a greater understanding of how and when these "issues" became a burden in your life and caused you to get stuck and, also they are coming up so that you can release the specific blockage to the Lord.

Then as you say to the Lord, "I give all of this to you, see "it," the influence of the memory, leaving you and going to Jesus. You may need to verbally forgive anyone that has been part of your memory experience by simply saying with all your heart, "Lord, I forgive ....and ask you to forgive them." As you do this, realize that to forgive actually means to pardon...to allow that person to go free. He will deal with it from there as He desires!

Then, very important; ask Him to fill those places emptied of the pain with His love and truth about what His purposes were for you then and are for you now. This is such a powerful part of the process because if your memory, for instance, was from a time when you were younger, that "little person," that is still very much emotionally a part of who you are today, needs to realize that in spite of what happened, they were always loved by the Lord. You can ask Jesus to fill you (the wounded part of you) with the sense of well-being. Do not hurry. Take time to feel His Presence and experience His love as He takes away years of pains and hurts! This process is often like peeling an onion, it comes off one layer at a time!

As you go through this process on a regular basis, you will experience more and more freedom and all of the wounded parts of your personality can be healed and restored to a feeling of wholeness.

From testimonies we have received from individuals we have taken through this process, and from what we have experienced ourselves, this time of reflection and release can do more good than years of psychological counseling because it releases the root cause of so many problematic issues and allows truth and well-being to come in. The work Jesus does in your life is at the root level thus allowing new seeds of truth to replace the bitter roots that have been removed.

I heard a psychologist, who had learned a similar process, say that EVERY DAY he would sit with his children and ask them if there were any issues that had happened to them during the day that they would like to talk about, understand or release. How powerful is that for these children to grow up with a "clean house" so they do not have to "undo" stuff as they grow up.

A SIMILAR PROCESS WAS USED BY THE APOSTLE PAUL. IN FACT, HE SAID, THIS "ONE" THING I DO, I LET GO OF THE PAST ISSUES THAT ARE BLOCKING ME SO THAT I CAN PRESS FORWARD TO THE HIGH CALLING OF GOD IN CHRIST JESUS.

The Apostle Paul said in **Philippians 3:13**, "This ONE thing I do, forgetting those things that are behind, I press toward the mark of the high calling of God in Christ Jesus."

He did not say, He forgot! He said, "I am making it a part of my life to continue to forget (forgetting) those things that were in my past that are trying to hinder my movement forward. The original meaning of "forget" in the Greek language is "to lose out of mind!" Even the Apostle Paul had to get rid of past painful thoughts so that he could fulfill the high calling of God. We are all a work in progress and must maintain this attitude as well if we are to have the true success in life and reach our "mark of high calling" that God intends for us.

Again, do take a look at your life on a daily basis! If you have the same uncomfortable situations continually occurring such as problems because of feelings of rejection, resentment, frustration, hopelessness, anger, hostility, relationship failures, financial disruptions and failures, continue to ask Jesus to show you where the problem began or where the root is so "it" can be released and, just like the Apostle Paul, loosed out of your mind. .

It is very important to look at how we have related to our earthly parents or authority figures that have had an influence on us through the years. We must forgive our earthly fathers and mothers or anyone who has hurt us for the love they were not able to give. They may have already passed on but verbally releasing them releases you. Then, ask the Lord to cleanse your memories, "which is losing it out of your mind," so that you are free to accept His love as a caring Heavenly Father and move forward in life unimpeded by those issues.

This defeat cycle that sets so many up for ongoing wounded lives can be fixed. It is not a matter of blaming someone else for the pain they caused, but a truthful awareness of what has been passed on so that future generations will not go through another painful cycle of events.

ARE YOU WILLING TO BE WILLING?

If you are willing to take the time to pray a prayer of forgiveness, this will free you to accept your Heavenly Father's love. Just say, "Lord, I forgive (names) for the love they were not able to give to me. Thank you for cleansing my memories so that I am free to accept your love, Heavenly Father, and also free to receive the love of those you send my way, in Jesus Name! (You may need to take time to allow these memories to come up so that you can release them with the process mentioned above.)

This step is so important because we can represent the love of God to others only as much as we receive it ourselves. God wants you to be free to accept His love.

When God, by the Holy Spirit, can shine His love in your heart, then you will be in a position to experience miracles, healings, deliverances and wholeness....You will begin to experience true peace and acceptance.

FOLLOWING IS A GREAT EXAMPLE OF ONE WOMAN'S CHANGED LIFE THAT GOT A WHOLE CITY TALKING—ABOUT JESUS!

One of the greatest examples in the Bible of a marvelously changed life is in **John 4**. It is the story of the woman at the well and is such a powerful picture of how Jesus wants to take the painful events of our lives, bring truth to them by letting us know why we act the way we act and by removing the cause of the events that have caused so many defeat cycles in our lives. Think about how many peoples' lives have been changed through history by this lady's transforming story.

Jesus took time with her, brought truth to her, healed her and sent her on her way full of excitement for life. He desires to do the same for you. Only a person who had been totally freed from rejection, shame, embarrassment and guilt could have gone back to the people who had used her, abused her and demeaned her, and looked them in the eyes and said, "Come see the man that told me everything I ever did"....and... He still loves me! He loves you too and will do the same for you! She was so convincing and free that these men came out to see this Man themselves. Her chat with Jesus brought her such freedom that she came back to the city "free indeed." It also says many more Samaritans of that city believed because of what she "testified."

DO YOU NEED TO TAKE TIME WITH JESUS AND ALLOW HIM TO SHOW YOU WHY YOU KEEP DOING THE THINGS YOU DO? REMEMBER, "HE IS THE SAME YESTERDAY, TODAY AND FOREVER." HE WANTS YOU FREE TOO!

I believe the reason she was so freely able to convince these men and the people in the city was because Jesus took time to show her "why" she had been acting the way she had and his unconditional love freed her from her emotional and physical weaknesses. She was then free to go and live the life He had intended from the beginning...not based on counterfeit love but unconditional love!

We must have an experience with the Father's true love just as she did. Remember when Jesus said, "If you have seen me, you have seen the Father." His unconditional love was displayed to this woman that allowed her to feel loved and accepted—free from feelings of rejection that had obviously tormented and driven her life in wrong directions and caused her to make the same mistakes over and over again.

What would your life be like if you really realized God created you personally to love, and for His love and desires you to be free from the results of counterfeit and conditional love that you may have experienced?

Just as the woman at the well needed truth, freedom, and healing brought to her, you and I, if we are going to have a powerful influence must get the understanding about how much we are loved and accepted. Jesus came to show that love.

The key to your wholeness and happiness is in getting your heart and emotions healed... removing lies and replacing them with truth! Jesus went about doing good and healing all that were oppressed by the Devil....because God's love was with Him and in Him. He wants to do the same for you.

Remember again in **III John**, it says, "I wish ABOVE ALL THINGS that you would prosper and be in health, even as your soul prospers." Success in life, as God intended, is dependent on soul prosperity. When we get "born-again" our spirit is restored to God and given the gift of everlasting life; however, our success in life in the here and now is dependent on a renewed mind which accepts the truth of who we are and can become in Christ.

2 Corinthians 10:3 "For though we live in the world, we do not wage war as the world does. The weapons we fight with are not the weapons of the world. On the contrary, they have Divine Power to demolish strongholds. We demolish arguments and every pretension that sets itself up against the knowledge of God and we take every thought captive to make it obedient to Christ."

ACCORDING TO THIS, MANY THINGS THAT HAVE HAPPENED TO YOU HAVE BEEN "SET UPS" SO THAT A STRONGHOLD OR WALL WOULD BE PUT AROUND YOUR LIFE TO INHIBIT YOU FROM BRINGING GLORY TO GOD AND LIVING THE LIFE HE INTENDED FOR YOU. HE WANTS YOU TO WAGE A WAR AGAINST THESE ONSLAUGHTS BY KNOWING THE TRUTH AND APPLYING IT TO EVERY AREA OF LIFE!

Chapter 19
Are you captive to your thoughts?

THOUGHTS ARE THINGS! THINK ABOUT
ALL THE THOUGHTS YOU ARE CARRYING
AROUND WITH YOU NOW THAT MAY NEED
TO BE TAKEN CAPTIVE AND RELEASED.

We are told to take captive every thought: What is a thought? Thoughts are things. Thought in the Hebrew means to act as a janitor, a gatekeeper, and one that computes. According to the above Scripture, thoughts are so serious that if one creeps into our life, we are told to take "it" captive, demolish "it" before "it" builds a stronghold in our life and then replace it with what God has to say about "it." Realize too that you have to be aware that your thoughts are actually "arguing" with you but you must win over them with what the Word of God has to say about them! This Scripture is saying that our victory in life depends on our thoughts obeying what Christ says about us and has in mind for us!

Although we have listed quite a few events and relationship issues previously, it is important for the purpose of "more food for thought" to go over some situations again that can play a vital part in bringing you into more freedom so that you can enjoy life more fully.

We, in our early childhood, have not known how to take thoughts and words captive and, again, if our parents and their parents didn't understand this fact, the generational lies and negative patterns have been transferred to you and are stored in your mind and emotions ready to be triggered by an event at any moment. If your parents did not have a sense of God's unconditional love when you were born, you more than likely picked up their scars, fears and wounded emotions. God does not want you to remain emotionally handicapped.

People who did not learn or experience basic trust early in life, often develop fear and the need to control and it becomes a way of life. Lack of family love and unity has caused people to develop depraved minds. A depraved mind is one that is unable to accept the truth that God loves them and cares for them and has predestined good things for them. Therefore, they often try to control their environment in ungodly manipulating ways which ultimately causes more pain and destruction.

God wants to meet your deepest love need so that you are free to accept yourself and the love from others He sends your way. Thank God He has always planned new beginnings!

It is vital that you realize that people that have used you and hurt you misrepresented God's love. When you come to the realization that no human can meet your needs, only God's love filling those empty places, your destiny will be changed and your feelings of well-being will surface.

Psalms 22, says, "It was God that brought you forth! God was there creating you."

Your parents are the means He used to get your spirit to earth in a human body; His Son, Jesus, is the means He uses to get you back to Him!

YOU HAVE BEEN GIVEN A POWERFUL GIFT.....FREE CHOICE. YOU CAN BEGIN TO GET FREE FROM WRONG CHOICES SO THAT YOU CAN MAKE RIGHT CHOICES FROM NOW ON.

God has always been there with you; however, He gave people free choice. Their free choice spilled over to your free choice and the effects of their actions affected how you feel about yourself which is most often the reason you make the same mistakes over and over again. Experiencing the love of your Heavenly Father and learning and experiencing the great work Jesus accomplished for you will set you on a "course correction" that will bring glory to God and enable you to more fully enjoy life!

God wants you to be free from the things you have experienced that have led you to continue in wrong choices. Understanding the love involved in letting man have free choice can free you from many misconceptions and stored anger because of the wrong actions of others that have affected your life. God has always planned a way out for those that choose His love.

Jesus knew you would not be able to carry all of these cares and anxieties and that is one reason He came to earth, to take those cares from you. That is why He said to cast ALL of your cares on Him BECAUSE He cares for you.

This is a big key to experiencing emotional health:

God's wants you to experience and feel His care. Once you have experienced God's love and are released from strongholds around your mind, you will also have a greater compassion for those around you going through difficulties because you will realize from your own personal experience that somewhere along the line they, just as you, experienced painful events that altered their ability to live and love as God would have desired. You have no idea how freeing that can be until you experience it for yourself.

I once heard an evangelist say something that I have never forgotten, He said, "if you do not deal with the "stuff" in your life, the "stuff" will deal with you."

If you are truly tired of "stuff" dealing with you, I encourage you to take time to go back over the feelings associated with "bitter roots" and "oppressive" feelings and allow the Lord to bring up people, places or things that were involved with your negative hurtful memories, then release or give them to Jesus so that those places can be filled with His truth and love. He is waiting for you to choose to "Cast your cares on Him!"

HAVE YOU BEGUN TO GET A NEW HIGHER PERSPECTIVE ON WHAT TRUE LOVE REALLY IS?

Do you desire to experience a new perspective on what true love is? The high price has already been paid by the Lord Jesus for you to have life and have it MORE ABUNDANTLY! **John 10:10**

The character of the One who wants to love you as you deserve to be loved has been presented in this book. I have also included a **Life Shaping Prayer Method** that can be used to assist you in applying these principles to your life. My prayer is that the revelations of His True Love expressed in this book, that have already set so many individuals free to be able to live the life they were meant to live, will assist you in discovering how much you are loved, accepted and deemed a person of value by your Heavenly Father and that you, too, will begin to experience the good, acceptable and perfect will of God for you!

Thank you for reading this book, I encourage you to pursue Him in all you do and may God bless you on your journey of discovery to find God's true love revealed to you.

Diana M. Sykes

The Life-Shaping Prayer Method
(Personal Use Only)
BY
Gerald & Diana Sykes

This is an extremely simple Life-Shaping Prayer Method. The techniques shown can be very useful to bring a major transformation in your life if used on a regular basis.

It is intended to be used for your PERSONAL USE ONLY.

FOLLOWING IS HOW THE METHOD WORKS:

1. You have an ongoing "issue" come up that you need to understand or you need an answer as to why it continues to be problematic.

2. The next step:

An Opening Prayer:
Jesus, I give you the freedom and liberty to bring Truth and Healing to these areas of my life that I need answers to today.

Declaration:
I bind any demonic influence in my life and ask the True
Lord Jesus to deal directly with any such influence. Now,
Jesus I thank you for what you are going to do in my life today.
AMEN.
*(This Declaration is based on the authority given to you by Jesus to refuse
the works of the Devil in your life. "True Love Revealed" has endeavored
to show you a clear distinction between what God desires for you and
what the Devil and his oppressive system want for you.)*

3. Speak out the issue-question and turn the issue-question into an emotion. HOW DOES THAT EMOTION MAKE YOU FEEL?.... SAD, ANGRY, A FAILURE, CONFUSED, DISAPPOINTED, ETC.

(FOR INSTANCE, YOUR ISSUE IS THAT YOU DREAD SOCIAL SETTINGS EVEN THOUGH THESE COULD ENHANCE YOUR BUSINESS/SOCIAL LIFE. THIS MAKES YOU FEEL INFERIOR, EMBARRASSED AND SUBSEQUENTLY ANGRY BECAUSE OF MISSED OPPORTUNITIES.)

4. Ask Jesus to show you where or when that emotion first began.
THIS IS VERY IMPORTANT BECAUSE EMOTIONS AND WOUNDED FEELINGS ACCUMULATE AND BECOME LIKE WEEDS THAT GROW VERY RAPIDLY. YOU MUST FIND OUT WHERE THE ROOT BEGAN IN ORDER TO GET TRULY FREE.

5. Once Jesus has shown you where it first began, ESTABLISH WHAT AGE YOU WERE.

(MORE OFTEN THAN NOT, THE AGE WILL BE WHEN YOU WERE YOUNG; HOWEVER, THAT IS NOT ALWAYS THE CASE.)

6. You may experience the memory of an event, colors, smells, or a combination as Jesus builds a scenario for your healing.

7. Do not hurry. Be aware that the TRUTH concerning the reasons for the emotional situation may come to you at any time during the session.

8. One of the first things you may experience is ANGER and that is OK! Jesus is dealing with things that need to be released and flushed out.

9. Allow Jesus to take ALL of those emotions/feelings from you and replace them with His truth. His truth may differ greatly from what you have believed.

10. Once you know where the emotion-issues began, see (picture) yourself releasing the hurts, pains, rejections, disappointments and failures, whatever they are. See yourself hand them over to -
Jesus, one at a time and name them, Jesus I give you xxxxxx. THIS IS ONE OF THE MAIN HEALING MOMENTS AND IT IS VITAL TO BECOMING FREE! TAKE TIME!

11. Allow Jesus time to bring all of those areas that have been locked in time that HAD BEEN carrying all the pain and misconceptions to the PRESENT YOU. Allow Him time to do it!

REMEMBER, IT PROBABLY WILL BE EARLY YEARS OF
YOUR LIFE THAT HAVE CARRIED THE PAIN, BURDEN,
GUILT, ETC., BUT ALSO REMEMBER THAT IS NOT
ALWAYS THE CASE.

12. Now that you know the real TRUTH about the areas and questions that have caused you distress, you can encourage yourself by saying such things as, "Things are better now."

USE YOUR NAME OR NICKNAME AS IF SPEAKING
TO A THIRD PERSON. THOSE PARTS OF YOU WILL
BE SO RELIEVED TO HEAR AND FEEL THE TRUTH!

13. A major battle just took place! You and Jesus WON. EVEN IF YOU DON'T FEEL IT RIGHT NOW, IT HAPPENED!

14. The final step:

A Closing Prayer:
Thank you Jesus for the work you have done in my life today. I ask you to continue the work in the days and months ahead.

Amen

Disclaimer:
This Life-Shaping Prayer Method outlined above is not counseling.
It is at your option that you either accept or reject any truths and/or
thoughts that come to you as a matter of following the above
guidelines. No liability is accepted whatsoever by the Author.

Help & Questions
Contact: Gerald & Diana Sykes
E-Mail: Edreamshapers@aol.com
Website: www.Dreamshapers.net

Material is copyrighted and may not be distributed without prior
consent from Dreamshapers. Extracts can be used without consent.

SALVATION PRAYER

If you have never accepted Jesus Christ as your personal Savior,
may I encourage you to pray the following prayer:

Jesus, I ask you to come into my life
and to forgive me for all of my sins.
I confess with my mouth that you are Lord
and I believe in my heart that God
raised you from the dead that I might
experience life in all of its fullness.
I declare that I am now born again.

If you prayed this prayer, welcome into the family of God.
You have just made the most important decision of your life!

ROCKET YOUR FAITH

For your convenience and personal growth,
the following books are available from Diana M. Sykes:

True Love Revealed
This book leads you through a personal
journey of discovery and freedom.

Price $9.95 + Shipping and Handling $3.95

* * * * * *

Power Thoughts for Triumphant Living
A collection of power thoughts to recharge your
thoughts and reenergize your faith and an ideal book
for a fast pick-me-up. A great tool for group use!

Price $9.95 + Shipping and Handling $3.95

Internet Orders can be made online through:
www.barnesandnoble.com
www.amazon.com

Books are also available from:
Author Direct at
**P.O. Box 7869 Charlotte, NC 28241-7869
United States**

Please enclose a Check made to the order of:
DSInvestments

*Please remember to specify the title and
number of books that you require.*

For bulk purchases, please contact
Edreamshapers@aol.com directly.